Essential Youth

Why your church needs
young people

ANDY HICKFORD

KINGSWAY PUBLICATIONS
EASTBOURNE

ISBN 0 85476 661 8

23/7/98
PRESENT FROM RALPH & JANET SOAR
GRADUATION - OASIS YOUTH MINISTRY COURSE.

Designed and produced by Bookprint Creative Services
P.O. Box 827, BN21 3YJ, England, for
KINGSWAY PUBLICATIONS
Lottbridge Drove, Eastbourne, East Sussex BN23 6NT.
Printed in Great Britain.

Contents

Acknowledgements

Special thanks to those who have helped me write this book, especially to Heather Evans, Chris Russell and Martyn Smith for their comments on the first draft – all the best bits are theirs!

I am also indebted to Heather Corry for her extraordinary patience as she typed the manuscript again and again and who was such an encouragement when I doubted the wisdom of the venture.

Finally to my wife Cerys without whose incredible support the book would not have been possible.

Essential Youth is dedicated to the staff and members of Stopsley Baptist Church, Luton (1986–1996). It was with them that I learned about the essentialness of youth.

About the Author

Andy Hickford is the Pastor of Maybridge Christian Fellowship in Worthing. For ten years he was Youth Minister at Stopsley Baptist Church in Luton. A popular speaker and writer, he is married to Cerys and they have three children.

Foreword

I see no hope for the future of our people if they are
dependent on the frivolous youth of today, for certainly
all youth are reckless beyond words.... When I was
young we were taught to be discreet and respectful of
elders, but the present youth are exceedingly impatient of
restraint. (Hesiod, Greek poet, eighth century BC)

This view is not unknown in church life today!
Thousands of young people have felt the church to be
only distantly related to reality and very closely
related to irrelevance. They have felt divorced from the
decision-making, alienated from the worship and
excluded from the heart of church life.

But this is not the whole story. Some young people
feel loved and secure in their churches; and they
participate in well run, dynamic youth activities.

This book will encourage all churches to do
thoughtful youth work. It will challenge the trio of
views which in some measure characterise so many of
our churches. Young people are patronised, ignored or
idolised – all to the detriment of both the young people
and church life as a whole. *Essential Youth* will help a
church reach and keep young people.

But I believe that *Essential Youth* does far more than
this. It argues vigorously for a model of church life
which takes young people from the edge to the centre.
Our structures and strategies are then exposed to these
cultural insiders as they experience the full force of

7

adolescent post-modernity, and force us to grapple with their dilemmas. Confronted by these rude, direct challenges to our comfort zones, it's hard to imagine things staying the same!

Of course none of this implies that young people are perfect. Both Hesiod and Hickford recognise this reality! Nevertheless, between the naiveté which believes young people are always right and the arrogance which believes they are always wrong, lies the productive possibility of tapping into the 'wisdom of innocence'.

This book longs to see a rigorous re-appraisal of the effectiveness of church life. It calls us to listen to those who 'feel' cultural relevance almost instinctively as well as to those who try to understand it intellectually. Young people are the church of yesterday. Let's listen to them today, so that we can be helped to be the best church we can for tomorrow.

Stephen Gaukroger

Author's Preface

I first met James when he was twelve years old. I noticed him because it was snowing and he was standing outside the local Co-op in only a tee-shirt. He was frozen. We got chatting and I gave him a lift home. That was the start of a friendship which was to last over ten years.

Of all the young people I have ever worked with, it is James who has made me struggle the most with what it means to share Jesus with someone of a different background. For without doubt, though he only lived down the street from me, James and I came from different worlds. His dad was long-term unemployed and bordering on alcoholic. His mum was an acute agoraphobic who rarely left her living room. His older brother was in care and his two younger brothers were already in trouble with the police. His whole outlook on life was entirely different from mine.

He came round one Friday night, more excited than I had ever seen him before. 'Look what I've found,' he said. In his hand was a small wage packet that he had picked up outside a building site on his way home from school. I counted the money. There was £180. I took a deep breath and as gently as possible I said, 'James, you know what I think you should do with this money, don't you?'

His expression changed, he looked me straight in the eye and said quietly, 'And if you were a kid like me, you know what you'd do, don't you?'

I have to admit, I had nothing else to say. James never did get the money though. His dad took it off him that night and spent the whole lot in one trip to the off-licence.

With those words though, James had unwittingly focused my task as a Christian youth worker. 'If you were a kid like me' – that was exactly what I needed to do. To start thinking like James did, see the world through his eyes, put myself in his position and begin to try to feel how he must feel. If I were a kid like James, what would doing well at school mean? If I were a kid like James, what would honouring my parents mean? If I were a kid like James, what would fulfilling my potential mean? And supremely, what would it mean to follow Jesus?

Without fully appreciating what was happening, I had started along the road of trying to place the gospel in the context of the people I was working with. In reality, I was setting off in hot pursuit along a track well worn by many a missionary before me.

Little did I know then that over the next ten years James was to teach me more than I was able to teach him. While I tried to help him understand the gospel, James helped me to understand it in ways I had never seen before. While I was trying to help James overcome his background, he helped me overcome mine. While I was trying to help James relate to church, he helped me to see the role of the church more clearly than I had ever seen it before. While I prayed for James to experience Jesus, through working with James I began to understand more of how Jesus wanted to work in my own life.

Evangelism to others also became a process of God's

revelation to me. Meeting James and kids like him was to change my understanding of Christian ministry.

To read this book, then, is to join in that same journey of discovery that working with young people can provide. *Essential Youth* is all about how the church can learn about itself and the nature of the gospel in today's world by working with and listening to teenagers. It's about the problems we face as a church and how working with young people can help solve them.

Essential Youth is organised in three sections, but it is only in the last section that some of the specific lessons we can learn are actually dealt with. Why? Because to get to that point we must first do our biblical thinking. In times of change it is more important than ever to keep coming back to the Bible for the principles of what we should be doing. After all, we can only learn from young people if they reveal God's truth to us.

Section One is therefore all about culture and the vital role it plays in both understanding the Christian message and living out the Christian faith. Here we see that today's church has big problems with culture and that we can only begin to see our immediate world, as God would have us see it, with the help of people from different cultures and backgrounds from our own.

Section Two looks at whether young people today can really be said to be people of a different culture. At first it sounds a bit over the top; after all, they live in the same street and speak the same language as we do. However, it's an important section for this reason: if it is valid to see them as a separate cultural group, then it is also valid that God can use them to show us things about our churches that we fail to see at the moment.

Finally, we get to Section Three and the lessons we

can learn. Today's church is really struggling with contemporary culture, yet it has in its midst people who belong to that culture and who can be employed in helping the church engage that culture. These people are the youth of our churches. The world needs them. The church needs them, and for everybody's sake we need them now.

Andy Hickford

SECTION ONE

Cultural Captives

Youth work is essential to the church because it forces us to take seriously the issue of culture.

I

Why Do We Do That?
(Culture defined)

I'm confused! When I was young, tattoos were the exclusive domain of hairy bikers and rugged sailors! But now it seems they have become the latest hot fashion accessory. Young beautiful women want a tattoo. What is going on?

Think about your hair cut and why you have it the way you do. Ask yourself why you bought the clothes that you are wearing right now. Think about the music that you listen to or the food that you had for your last meal. Think about where you want to go on holiday next year or even whether you like tattoos or not. Think about these issues and you immediately start thinking about culture.

Culture is experienced more readily than it can be described. It is the air we breathe. It is the water we swim in. It is everything about our background and environment which shapes the people we are.

So, for example, you are not the first person to have your hair that way or to dress as you are today. In making those choices you were first influenced by the styles and fashions around you. You may not view yourself as a fashion victim, but the truth is that you only had a number of options to choose from and those options were shaped by the culture of which you are part. What do men wear in the West other than trousers? It is not like British Home Stores is doing a special promotion this year on loin cloths, is it? However outrageous the colour and cut you choose, when all is said and done they are all still trousers!

THIS YEAR BHS IS NOT DOING A
SPECIAL PROMOTION IN LOINCLOTHS...

The same is true for women. The very fact that women can choose to wear trousers if they want to, let alone have a tattoo, is in itself a cultural statement. In many countries women do not have the choice. You may not be a fashion victim, but we are all cultural creations.

'Culture is an integrated system of beliefs, values, customs and institutions which bind a society together and give it a sense of identity, dignity, security and continuity.' [1]

Shaped and changed by things like our history, technology, art and national identity, culture comes to define our ideas about what is right and wrong, good and bad, our tastes and preferences and our expectations about how we should behave.

So, then, culture is the context in which we live our daily lives. In short, 'It's the way we do things round here!' [2]

Cultural specs

It was the great missionary writer, Lesslie Newbigin, who first seized upon the illustration of glasses to describe how culture's influence affects us all. He said that without realising it our culture issues us with a pair of spectacles through which we see and understand the world. Other writers have called these specs our worldview.

Mike Starkey put it like this: 'My worldview is the pair of mental spectacles through which I view everything, it is the unifying vision which not only affects how I see the world, it even affects what I see there, highlighting some things and masking others, revealing some things as desirable, others to be avoided.... We all wear a pair of worldview spectacles (whether we know it or not), and none of us could operate without them.' [3]

Invisible power

Culture exerts massive influence on every individual human being through these specs. In many ways, culture defines what is possible.

SEEING THE SPECS

One day my worst fears were realised as I tentatively opened the fridge door and, much to the amusement of my undergraduate friends, found that the entire contents of my underwear drawer were now a solid block of ice in the freezer compartment! I was just wondering what I was going to do while my pants defrosted, when one of the African students strode in. He very angrily seized all his food from the fridge and threw it in the bin. Then he proceeded to demand compensation from my friends for making his lunch 'unclean'!

A little put out, I quickly assured him that my pants had only just been washed, but it was no good, I was obviously missing the point entirely. This was a cultural thing. He could not 'hear' my explanations about student humour. Underwear and food were kept separate where he came from(!) and he wanted his money back. In the circumstances I thought it was only fair to try to make sure that my friends paid up!

Culture can only exercise this kind of power, though, because it goes unnoticed. It is powerful precisely because it is invisible.

It is the very normality of everything around us that seduces us into believing that culture does not affect us too much. In reality, entirely the opposite is true.

George Gerbner put it like this: 'What people learn best is not what their teachers teach, or what their parents preach, but what their cultures in fact cultivate.'[4]

Cultural essentials

For the Christian, discovering these cultural specs is very important. It helps us to understand the way we think and behave, it helps us recognise the pressures we live under and, most importantly, it helps clear away those areas of our life that Jesus wants to change.

> Don't become so well-adjusted to your culture that you fit into it without even thinking. Instead, fix your attention on God (Rom 12:2, *The Message*).[5]

> True conversion to Christ is bound, therefore, to strike at the heart of our cultural inheritance. Jesus Christ insists on dislodging from the centre of our world whatever idol previously reigned there and occupying the throne himself.[6]

That is not to say that all of culture's influence is negative – some of it can be very positive. The point is that as Christians we need to recognise its influence in the first place!

Sadly, however, for the majority of Christians the issue of culture still remains largely hidden, the glasses undiscovered.

To sum up so far: culture's influence in shaping the way we think and behave is enormous and at the same time profoundly unnoticeable!

2

Trapped

(The church's problem with culture)

Introduction

Culture's power to influence our lives without us realising it has big consequences for the church. On the one hand, our evangelism struggles to break free from the church's own culture in order to reach the world. On the other, our discipleship often fails to break out of the world to be God's church. It sounds absurd, but the church today is largely a cultural captive.

I am suggesting in this book that by making work with young people a priority, we discover, almost by accident, keys to unlock this situation. But first, let's look in more detail at the nature of the captivity. What follows is a summary of a number of writers on where many Christians find themselves today.

Cultural discipleship

> The first call of the gospel of Christ is not to proclamation... nor is it social action. The first call of the gospel of Christ is incarnation – living out something that is radically different.[1]

Discipleship is following Jesus, the process by which

we become more like Christ. It is about learning to see the world as God sees it; it is about developing biblical thinking; it is about starting to relate to people and our environment as Jesus would. To be a disciple is to be a pilgrim, journeying through this world, living in anticipation of the next, bringing the future into the present, dancing to a different rhythm and marching to a different drum beat from that of the world.

The great danger on this journey is that when we are not sufficiently aware of our own cultural specs, we confuse our culture's values with what we think are Christian values. So, for example, even one of the great evangelists like D. L. Moody made the mistake of labelling the four great sins of his day as the theatre, Sunday newspapers, evolution and a disregard for the Sabbath![2] One can't help thinking that he had missed a few! Moody had allowed his cultural specs to colour his understanding of true discipleship.

Often still today our cultural blindness goes right to the heart of what it means to be a Christian. In recent years there have been several areas in which we in the West have begun to see that our imitation of Christ is clearly compromised by our culture.

RATIONAL FAITH

Rationalism is the idea that the only things worth knowing are the things that we can think about and understand. With human reason as its idol rationalism has been one of the foundational pillars of the modern Western world.

Christians growing up in this environment very readily picked up on a strand of the Bible's teaching about loving God with our minds (Mt 22:37), thinking with renewed minds (Rom 12:2), and setting our minds on things above (Col 3:2) – not just because it was biblical, but because it was part of the modern Western culture. It led to great advances in Christian scholarship which have been of tremendous value to the church, but for some, loving God with our minds became limiting him with them instead. That which they could not fully understand and find a proof text for was either ignored, or dismissed as unbiblical. In doing so, Christianity was trapped in rational culture.

FEELING FAITH

Rationalism became so claustrophobic that it provoked a huge reaction in the Western world which has become known as post-modernism.

'Post-modernism is a reaction against modernism, which had reason with a capital R.'[3]

Once again the church mirrored this cultural shift. Christians growing up in these generations have less of a problem accepting a supernatural God who is to be experienced and whose infinite ways and thoughts are beyond our finite understanding (Is 55:8; 1 Cor 2:9–10). Once again, though, there was an over-reaction. As a young teenager in the heady days of charismatic renewal, I was told on many occasions, 'Don't think – feel!' No longer was rational thought the foundation of faith – experience was!

Both rational and feeling faith have cut and pasted the Bible. God's word holds the two in perfect tension. He is to be worshipped and known in both thought and experience (1 Cor 14:15–20). Nevertheless, both forms of culturally compromised Christianity are alive and depressingly well within evangelicalism today.

'Beware of cultural captivity. Study today's philosophy and tomorrow's theology will come as no surprise. The former queen of the sciences has lost her throne and is now working as a fashion model.'[4]

PRIVATE FAITH

Another cultural pressure which imperceptibly pushed Christianity in an unbiblical direction was the privatising of faith. As society became more multi-cultural, there evolved a way of living together which avoided constant arguing about religion. Over time, there emerged in our culture a distinction between the private and public worlds of faith. Religious faith became respected and valued when practised by individuals, but unwelcome and opposed if that private faith 'strayed' into the public domain with implications for others.

Christians brought up in this culture were able to see the strand of biblical teaching which emphasised the devotional aspects of discipleship, such as worship, prayer and Bible study, and got into them in a big way, spawning in the process a whole industry of conferences, books and resources. But the truth is that they did so not just because the Bible says they are important, but because the culture said that it was OK. If push came to shove, these generations of Christians might indulge in the occasional time of personal evangelism, but to suggest, for example, that to be salt and light in our world means Christians should be politically active is entirely alien to their thinking.

Private faith has also meant that Christian teaching on holiness has tended to be preoccupied with our 'private' lives:

> By focussing their attention on gambling or drink, [Christians] ignore the way in which they have unconsciously absorbed their neighbours' views on virtually everything else. They strain at a gnat and swallow a whole cultural camel.[5]

...STRAIN AT A GNAT AND SWALLOW A WHOLE CULTURAL CAMEL.

So today the public world is a world of 'facts', a world dominated by politics and business. It is an aggressive, critical world; an environment in which there are many who would seek to oppose and discredit Christianity, as well as offer alternatives.

The private world is a world of values, a world of no rights and no wrongs, a world which is cosy and safe and where respect for personal choice reigns. In the late twentieth century, evangelicalism has often retreated here and is only just beginning to realise that we must break out. It is strange when you think about it. The Romans persecuted Christians precisely because they refused to retreat to the private world. They believed that if Christ was true, he was truth for the whole empire. How times change!

As with animals, so for the Church. The price of conservation is captivity.[6]

'What once turned the world upside down has now turned in on itself.'[7]

MATERIAL FAITH

Storing up for ourselves 'treasures on earth' is hardly a new issue. Even in the third century Cyprian was stark about this area of cultural captivity for Christians: 'Their property held them in chains, chains which shackled their courage and choked their faith, hampered their judgment and throttled their souls.'[8]

This same cultural entrapment continues, however. Our calling to 'simplicity, generosity, and contentment' as John Stott has put it[9], seems to be comprehended only by a minority. We still assume that as we get older and progress, we will try and buy bigger houses, better cars, have more holidays and acquire all the necessary accessories for a comfortable lifestyle. The thought that in a world of limited resources this means that the poor will always stay poor and that such ambition is culturally not biblically driven, never enters our head.

As Tom Sine put it: 'Many of us have unquestionably attempted to layer our faith right over the top of the secular values with which we have been raised. We have simply accepted cultural expectations (such as looking after Number One) as largely unquestioned givens.'[10]

We have not recognised the exclusive nature of discipleship. We have taken on cultural baggage and tried to Christianise it. The agenda has been set and we've tried to add a nice God-type 'any other business' at the end, when all the time Christians should refuse to accept the agenda in the first place. We have tried to see where Jesus might fit into everything when actually it is where everything fits into Jesus that is the real question.

'God wants to start messing around with our cultural values, to transform our life direction from upwardly mobile to outwardly ministering.'[11]

Culture's influence on our attempts to follow Christ is

a real problem. The crisis in the church is one of product quality. The question at the heart of discipleship is: Where are we going to get our values from – our culture or Jesus? When our imitation of Christ is compromised by our material, private, rational and feeling faith we are no different from anybody else. The dreadful truth is that we don't really have that much to offer.

'Show the world a real, living, self sacrificing, toiling, triumphing, hard working religion and the world will be influenced by it. Anything less than that and they will turn round and spit on it.'[12]

Cultural evangelism

Blindness to our cultural conditioning becomes even more destructive when it comes to evangelism. Nowhere is this more clearly seen than in foreign mission experience. Well-meaning but culturally ignorant missionaries often wreaked havoc on a country's culture in the name of the gospel. In the name of Christ, missionaries shipped out to Africa organs and choir robes for people of the drum and the loin cloth.

Today the same forces of ignorance are at work in evangelism on our doorsteps. We are once again failing to take due consideration of the people we are trying to reach. In our enthusiasm to explain that Jesus is the answer, we overlook the fact that nobody is asking the question. We are occasionally in touch with our culture, but nearly always out of tune with it. As a TV producer said to Steve Chalke, 'You evangelicals are always trying to answer question number 17, when we are not even sure what question number 1 is. You need

...WE OVERLOOK THE FACT THAT NOBODY IS ASKING THE QUESTION

to begin where we are, not where you want us to be. Some of you are worse than politicians. It makes no difference what the question is, you always tell us what you want us to hear anyway.'[13]

With the vast majority of the country not Christian, we have to ask ourselves whether people consciously reject Christ or whether it is more subtle than that. 'Is it because they were being offered something they did not realise they needed, in a vocabulary that they did not comprehend, by someone who seemed indifferent from the needs they knew they had?'[14]

The problem is more than one of communication. Our cultural entrapment is more serious than that. The real problem in evangelism is that the church is communicating exactly what it is – out of touch. Essentially we can't engage with our world today because the Christian culture we have developed around us alienates the church from normal people. We use different words, listen to different music, go to different places, read different books and now even go on different holidays!

So strong is this entrapment that writer Peter Wagner suggests that it only takes a convert five years in a church before he ceases to know any other non-Christians![15]

How badly we need to hear the words of wisdom written many years ago which take the issue of culture in evangelism seriously: 'Conversion involves repentance, but this does not require the convert to step right out of his former culture into a Christian sub-culture which is totally distinctive. Conversion is not migration, it is the personal discovery of the meaning of the universal Christ, within the old framework of race, language and tradition.'[16]

At the end of the day our primary concern must continue to be what God thinks of the church, not what society thinks of it. However, we place so many unnecessary obstacles in the way of people coming to faith that our practice of church urgently needs reviewing. Perhaps the greatest task facing Evangelicals at the end of the twentieth century is not so much to build bridges into the community, but rather to make those bridges unnecessary in the first place.

To do so, we will need to get out of the culture trap.

Summary of Chapter 2

Beware, you will need to read this carefully! Here is

the ultimate irony. Our culture has too much influence on our Christian discipleship, while at the same time not having enough influence on our church evangelism!

So we are caught between two unpalatable options: to be relevant but indistinctive, or distinctive but irrelevant! Little wonder then that the church has problems with culture!

In the next chapter we shall see that our own cultural entrapment can be both exposed and helped by working with people of a different culture.

3

Exposé

(How we are helped by working with different cultures)

⟶

I could not have come to this critical stance in relation to my own culture without the experience of living in another.[1]

Words failed to do justice to my embarrassment. In front of everybody in the room, Jim was now holding my hand, earnestly looking me in the eyes and singing to me! I wanted the ground to swallow me up, especially when another of my friends got out the video camera!

This incident makes no sense unless the circumstances are understood. It took place in the slums of Addis Ababa, Ethiopia. It was a classic clash of cultures. I had given Jim (short for Baroojimah) the gift of a hat and as he could not speak any English he communicated his gratitude in a way that was entirely in keeping with his culture – he sang to me! I was the only one in the whole room who appeared in any way uncomfortable. Everything about my background said that grown men did not sit next to each other holding hands, looking into each other's eyes and singing! It did not make what Baroojimah did wrong, of course. It was just that the cultures he and I had grown up in were so vastly different.

Takes one to know one

There is no clearer way of discovering what our cultural spectacles look like than when they are knocked askew by bumping into another culture. There is nothing like that culture jolt to let you see that you are a cultural product too and that your values, tastes and standards have all been shaped by your background as surely as your hosts' have.

This experience can be of even greater significance for the Christian. It is perhaps only in this cross-cultural encounter that we are almost forced to begin the difficult but vital task of evaluating what of our Christian practice is authentically Christian and what is of our culture. In other words, to begin the Romans 12 process of refusing to be squeezed into the world's mould.

Not that a 'freestanding' gospel completely separate from culture exists, because of course the original gospel was itself tied to the culture of its day. What we have to do instead is be as clear as we can about the biblical principles which apply to all cultures and the points where our own cultural bias affects our reading of Scripture.

Incident to insight

It was only slowly that I began to see that I too had in a measure co-opted Jesus into the world view of my culture. It was an incident in an Indian village which made me realise this. I was taking a group of village teachers through St Mark's gospel. My Tamil wasn't very good, but I was fairly confident about my theology, fresh as I was from theological college. All went well until we reached the first exorcism. Now Westminster College had not taught me much about casting out demons. My exposition was not very impressive. These village teachers looked at me with growing perplexity, and then one of them said, 'Why are you making such heavy weather of a simple matter?' and proceeded to rattle off half a dozen cases of exorcism in his own congregation in the past few months. Of course, I could have said, 'My dear brother, if you will let me arrange for you to come to Cambridge and take a proper training in modern science and then a post graduate psychology degree, you will discover that Freud and Yung have explained everything!' In other words, 'If you will permit me to induct you into my culture, you will see things as they really are.' But this was a Bible study and Mark's gospel was open before us, saying precisely what it does. Inwardly, I had to admit that he was much closer to the text than I was. Outwardly, I kept quiet and went on to the next passage![2]

So many of the great mission writers talk of these awkward encounters setting them off on their path to discovery about the nature of the gospel, that it is hard not to conclude that the more difficult the cultural challenge, the greater the insight into the gospel as a result.

I can still remember when I first tried to communicate the gospel to a Masai tribesman, sitting under a tree in his red blanket. He had never been more than a few miles from his home. But I could see in my conversation with him that he valued three things: that he could walk fifty miles a day; that he knew all that there was to know about his cows; and that he was a Masai, the most important people on the earth. He could see that I was not a Masai, that I did not know a thing about cows and that I could hardly walk ten miles. So to him I was completely valueless. He had an air of superiority that began to get to me. I asked myself, how can I communicate my very important message when he can't care less about anything I have to offer?[3]

So often as a youth worker I have gone through the same range of emotions and asked myself the same questions. Talking in night clubs to lads whose only interest was women, with boys at the park who just wanted to play football (and I was always rubbish at football!), with a group of travellers' kids who viewed me with utter bewilderment, with school groups and even kids at church, my question has so often been the same. How can I communicate my very important message when they couldn't care less about anything I have to offer?

Every time, though, I kept coming back to James, the lad I spoke of in my Preface. 'If you were a kid like me' kept on going around and around in my head.

One afternoon after school he came round to my flat. He looked so fed up I asked him what was wrong. 'The kids at school are calling me gypo because of my sad clothes,' he said. Now I had read the books on handling personal anger and helping people through rejection, so I said the right thing, 'And how did that make you feel, James?'

'Dunno,' came the reply, 'I just threw a brick at them!'

At this point in our relationship the generational tensions were less than they were to become later. Initially the gap between us had its root in class, family, education and wealth. At twelve he knew I was not just older – we were different. With hindsight, I see now that even before I met him, James had lost hope, he knew he was a failure. Life was not about dreams but existence. He was already angry.

As I spent time with James I slowly began to realise how deep the differences between us went. To do well at school for me had meant going to university, for James it meant not getting permanently excluded. To eat well had meant for me having a balanced diet of three square meals a day. For James it meant having some change in his pocket for chips. 'Going home' was for me a safe and peaceful place. For James there was no place of peace in his life. The best bit of Christmas for me was celebrating with all the family. For James it was being allowed to stay in bed all day and watch TV.

Eventually it dawned on me: if we were so very different, why was I trying to introduce James to Jesus the same way as Jesus had been introduced to me? Why did I expect that if James was to become a Christian he would follow Jesus like I did? Nothing else in our lives was the same so why should Christianity be any different? Of course, the principles would be consistent, but surely I had to expect the practice of faith to be very different?

So I started the process of unravelling my faith as a Christian, asking myself what was essential to be passed on to James and what was simply my culture's practice and therefore inappropriate to James' world. I was discovering what the missionaries had learnt before me. The best way to discover how our culture has unwittingly shaped our Christian faith is to try and pass on that faith to people of a different culture from our own.

Any amount of cross-cultural experience will fail to

deliver the church from its culture trap, however, unless it goes hand in hand with a clear understanding of the Bible's teaching on culture.

4

Back to the Book

(What the Bible teaches about culture)

Before we look at an overview of what the Bible teaches on culture, a word of warning. As we have already seen, we all come to the Bible biased. 'No one can escape sharing in the mentality and intellectual climate of his own culture.'[1]

Bearing this in mind, we must always be careful to try not to read into the Bible the prejudices of our own background. Instead, we need to try to interpret the Bible within its original culture and look for principles which still apply to us today.

Culture in the Old Testament

As early as Genesis 1:28–30, God appears to give man a cultural mandate to take the initiative in stewardship over his environment: 'Fill the earth and subdue it. Rule over the fish of the sea and the birds of the air and over every living creature.' From there on, there seems to be a strong theme in the Old Testament that God's people are not helpless victims of their circumstances, but can live according to different priorities. For example, Noah and his family were saved from the flood precisely because they were not like the rest of society, and God called Abraham to 'Leave your country, your people and your father's household and go to the land I will show you' (Gen 12:1).

Under the leadership of Moses and Joshua, God's people were wanderers, with no fixed cultural home. When they finally entered the promised land, they did so with clear instructions to behave very differently from its previous occupants: 'When you enter the land the Lord your God is giving you, do not learn to imitate the detestable ways of the nations there' (Deut 18:9). Indeed, they were commanded to remain distant from their neighbours (Exod 34:15).

Joseph, David, Daniel and Nehemiah are seen as heroes of the faith because they did not compromise their beliefs under the pressures of a foreign culture. At a personal level, in the wisdom literature of the Old Testament, there is often an appeal to the reader not to succumb to being like all the rest (Prov 7:25–26).

The ministry of the prophets also had this strong 'counter-culture' theme. When Israel conformed to the practices of the surrounding nations, by worshipping idols or looking to other nations instead of God for alliances and support, they were strongly condemned (Amos 3:4; Is 3:1–2).

Generally speaking, then, the Old Testament seems to have a 'come out and be separate' focus to its teaching on how God's people should relate to the world. However, that's not to say that culture should be understood entirely negatively in the Old Testament. After all, the story of the tower of Babel (Gen 11) seems to suggest that different cultures are part of the way God made humanity with a tendency to variety. In that sense God positively endorses culture. Perhaps because of this, even in the Old Testament, there does appear to be some overlapping of cultures, where God's purposes accommodate existing patterns of behaviour and thinking in the surrounding cultures. So, for example, polygamy (the practice of taking more than one wife), as practised by other nations, is taken up by the Israelites and not explicitly condemned in the Old Testament. Even

POLYGAMY WAS TAKEN UP BY THE ISRAELITES...

the fundamental concepts of covenant and God's laws have equivalent cultural parallels in the surrounding nations.[2] In fact, in 1 Kings 8, God even appears to concede to the request to give Israel a king so they could be like the other nations – despite the dire warnings of its cost from the prophet Samuel (1 Sam 8:19–20).

The New Testament

In the New Testament, however, while a strong

counter-culture theme continues (e.g. 1 Jn 2:15; Rom 12:1; Col 3:8–11) there does appear to be more positive interaction between the Christian gospel and the non-Christian cultures of the day.

THE MINISTRY OF JESUS

As Thom Hopler put it, 'Jesus crossed the cosmic culture barrier' and in doing so provided us with models for cross-cultural communication. For example, the Jews and Samaritans were bitter enemies to the extent that Jews would take long detours to avoid even travelling through Samaria. Not so Jesus. He went straight through the country and engaged an obvious outcast of even her own people in conversation (Jn 4:7ff). In doing so, Hopler suggests, Jesus provides us with four helpful principles for cross-cultural evangelism:

- honest acknowledgement of our background and how it shapes our beliefs (vv. 9, 19–20);
- overcoming prejudice and difficulty by careful listening (vv. 13–15);
- finding elements of truth in a different culture (v. 17b);
- challenging what is wrong (vv. 22–24).

From the dialogues of Jesus, it is also possible to see how the circumstances of an individual would to some extent at least shape what Jesus said to them. For example, in Luke 10:25–37 and Mark 10:17–25, the lawyer and the rich young ruler ask Jesus the same question, yet they receive different answers. Jesus appears to be very sensitive to the starting point of his listeners and determined to begin 'where they are'.

ACTS

But how would Christianity fare beyond the boundaries of Judaism? It is in the book of Acts that the gospel's interlacing with Greek and Roman culture becomes most intriguing.

'In terms of culture, Paul varied the approach. In Acts 14 in the pagan town of Lystra he spoke very differently to Antioch, which was Jewish (Acts 13) and again to the philosophical Greeks of Ephesus in Acts 19:10. Paul gives two insights: 1) that the cultural background of the recipient must determine what the communicator can present, at least initially. 2) Paul did not change the message, but rearranged the component parts.'[3]

Crossing entrenched cultural barriers with the gospel was a huge challenge, both to individual Christians and the wider church. Peter went through a personal crisis on more than one occasion, as God allowed the gospel gradually to dislodge his proud Jewish cultural specs (Acts 10 and 11; Gal 2:11ff.).

At the Council of Jerusalem in Acts 15, the church faced a huge dilemma. Jewish Christians were trying to establish what of their faith and practice was the gospel and what was their culture. What was of the gospel needed to be passed on to the new Gentile churches; what was of their particular Jewish culture did not. The outcome of this defining moment in church history leaves us today with excellent principles for church planting in different cultures:

- give teaching on clear principles (i.e. Acts 15:29);
- give room for on-the-ground interpretation (Acts 15:28);
- send people of faith to model the message (Acts 15:25).

PAUL SWOTS UP FOR ATHENS...

Paul's speech to the Areopagus in Acts 17 is perhaps the finest example of culturally attuned preaching in Scripture. In a basically hostile environment, in which Paul felt distressed, he nevertheless acknowledged the religious orientation of his listeners and then went on to explain the gospel using terms that they could understand. A knowledge of Old Testament scriptures could no longer be assumed of his audience, so he quoted from their own Greek poets. He never once compromised the gospel message, but rather made the unpalatable understandable. In effect, he was 'reloading' cultural terminology to draw out Christian truths. A skilled piece of cross-cultural communication if ever there was one.

Acts 17 leaves us with at least four principles for cross-cultural communication today:

- good communication is in the language of the receptor culture (v.28);
- good gospel communication truly engages the audience (v.32);
- true gospel communication will radically challenge any culture (v.24);
- true gospel communication will always carry with it the possibility of rejection (v.32).

In the New Testament epistles, there are examples of how the writers were applying the truth of the Christian gospel to the circumstances and culture of the churches to which they were writing, the rampant immorality of Corinth being the classic example of this. From the wider biblical material, at least two patterns emerge as to how the gospel interacts with culture.

In and out

It does appear that in both the New Testament and the Old Testament God often uses people who are in one culture and yet are not truly part of it – people who are in effect bi-cultural. For example, Moses was Hebrew, yet brought up Egyptian; Daniel and Nehemiah trained in Babylonia, but were Jewish. In the New Testament, Paul and Barnabas were clearly bi-cultural. Barnabas was a Levite, but from Cyprus, and Paul had impeccable credentials, both as a Jew and a Roman citizen (Gal 1:14; Acts 16:37).

In not of

The gospel touches down in the time and space of the Roman Empire, but it refuses to stay there. The gospel tackles the issues of the day in a way that genuinely engages the real world, but at the same time points beyond it.

So, for example, in the teaching of Ephesians 5 and 6, the gospel engages contemporary issues while at the same time bringing implications which go far beyond the norms of the day. Paul tackles everyday relationships, starting where the culture is: 'Slaves, obey your earthly masters' (6:5); 'Children, obey your parents' (6:1); 'Wives, submit to your husbands' (5:22). However, at the same time the apostle challenges the accepted customs of the culture: 'And masters, treat your slaves in the same way' (6:9); 'Fathers, do not exasperate your children' (6:4); 'Husbands, love your wives just as Christ loved the church and gave himself up for her' (5:25).

In short, a gospel which engages culture, yet at the same time transcends it. A gospel that is in the world, but not of it.

Balancing act

For Christians to deal biblically with the issue of culture, then, requires an exquisite sense of balance. By being either uncritically affirming or unnecessarily negative to the world, we fail to be fully Christian. The obvious danger lurking at every turn is that Christianity can be undermined by culture. The opportunity that opens up before us, though, is that Christianity can transform culture.

Summary

Biblically speaking, culture must be viewed as carrying within it the same inherent tensions as that of humanity. It bears the undeniable imprint of God ('the echoes of Eden', as Donovan put it) but at the same time it bears the corruption and selfishness of humanity (Rom 2:3).

'Because Man is God's creature, some of his culture is rich in beauty and goodness. Because he is fallen, all of it is tainted with sin and some of it is demonic.'[4]

The Evangelical Fellowship of the Anglican Communion has summed up this tension helpfully: 'All cultures have something God-given in them and have categories in which the gospel can begin to be understood. Yet every culture must be tested by scripture and is under the judgement of God.'

Biblically speaking though, there is one more piece to the jigsaw of how the gospel relates to culture, and that has to do with the nature of gospel truth itself.

5

To Humbly Go

(Grasping the truth about culture)

I thirst for truth, but shall not reach it until I reach the source.[1]

What we are able to learn from other cultures about our own faith and culture is almost entirely determined by our attitude to truth itself.

Truth is desperately important for us as Christians. We believe that God himself is Perfect Truth, that the Bible is inspired truth and that we are to walk in the truth. Christianity's claims to truth are also the hottest point of contention with a society today which has largely given up on truth's existence.

Because truth is so important and contentious, we must be careful to understand how we come to and hold on to a knowledge of the truth today.

Our starting point is that we can only know anything about God if he first chooses to reveal himself to us (Is 43:12; Rom 1:19). 'The secret things belong to the Lord our God, but the things revealed belong to us and to our children for ever' (Deut 29:29).

All truth, then, is a gift of grace – we only discovered it because God first chose to disclose it. True Christian knowledge should therefore be characterised by humility – not the strutting self-importance of so many in the academic world. Learning is a miracle of grace.

LEARNING IS A MIRACLE OF GRACE!

When that humility is lodged firmly in our minds, it changes the nature of our proclamation. The gospel itself is still clearly not negotiable (Jn 14:6), but our grasp and understanding of it is. We are finite minds struggling with the infinite: 'Now we see but a poor reflection as in a mirror; then we shall see face to face. Now I know in part; then I shall know fully, even as I am fully known' (1 Cor 13:12).

So we enter into conversations about our faith with confidence about truth revealed, but humble about truth expressed. We long for people to come to a saving knowledge of Christ for themselves, while at the same time we are very mindful that we know only in part, in all likelihood we have got some things wrong, and we have things to learn from those with whom we are talking. Such a view brings us to our knees. We have a gospel to tell which is a matter of life and death, but our mind cannot do justice to its dimensions! How desperately we need the Holy Spirit to lead us into all truth (Jn 16:13). Indeed, such is the emphasis in both the Old and New Testaments about humility and truth going together (Ps 25:9; Prov 11:2; Phil 2:3; Titus 3:2; Jas 3:13) that it is impossible to have truly Spirit-empowered mission without an attitude of humility towards the people we are wanting to reach.

When we have this more Christian attitude towards truth, we understand that God can work on us as well as through us in these encounters with people of other cultures. We are addressed in the gospel by one who is himself the truth. We do not possess 'it', he seeks to possess us. 'Christ speaks in this dialogue, revealing Himself to those who do not know Him and correcting the limited and distorted knowledge of those who do.'[2]

So can we remain truly biblical and yet still believe that truth about God can be found in other cultures and even other religions?

John Stott, in his book *Christian Mission in the Modern World*, sums up the biblical material in the following way: 'We therefore do not deny that there are elements of truth in non-Christian systems and vestiges of general revelation of God in nature. What we do deny is that these are sufficient for salvation.' John Stott goes on by quoting from the World Council of Churches at Uppsala:

The Christian's dialogue with another implies neither a denial of the uniqueness of Christ, nor any loss of his own commitment to Christ, but rather a genuinely Christian approach to others. He must be human, personal, relevant and humble. In dialogue we share our common humanity, its dignity and fallenness and express our common concern for that humanity.[3]

Here lies a critical point in this book. The church of Jesus Christ has been given the Great Commission, to take the good news of Jesus to every people group on the planet and to make disciples. In doing so, it must confront and challenge what is wrong in every society and stay faithful to the message of the cross. But it must also be prepared to learn. The sum total of God's revealed truth does not exclusively reside within the confines of the church (e.g. Gen 42) but in the one whom we worship, and he is not confined to the church.

Summary of Section One

We all tend to underestimate how powerful a hold culture has over us, and as far as the church is concerned, this attitude has devastating effects on both our discipleship and our evangelism.

Things do not need to remain as they are, however. By understanding the balance that the Bible teaches about culture, by having a more biblical appreciation of truth and by trying to reach people of a different culture with the gospel, our own cultural specs can be exposed, and a way out of the church's culture trap can be seen.

In Section Two we shall look at whether working with young people today can really be said to be working with people of a different culture. If it can, then of course young people can help lead the church out of its many and various cultural traps.

SECTION TWO

Young People – Are They Really a Different Culture?

Introduction

The world that shapes and influences teenagers of today is so vastly different from the world that shaped and influenced the average church leader, that to communicate between the two requires crossing a cultural chasm as broad and as difficult as that of the pioneers of Western mission in the last century.

Over the top? Can we really believe that teenagers today, living in the same town, speaking the same language, who are even part of the same family, should be understood as a different cultural group?

Well, let's see…

Beware of Monty Python!

One of my favourite comedy sketches is 'That's Nothing' by Monty Python. In it, each of the characters tries to outdo the other by exaggerating the level of their childhood poverty, with quite hilarious results.

When I read some articles today on contemporary culture, I think that the authors would do well to listen to Monty Python! It is as if today's young people are the only ones in the whole of history to live under the threat of physical violence, to be left picking up the pieces of their parents' foolishness and to struggle with confused signals from a society that has lost direction.

We are on very shaky ground if each generation of youth workers sees it as their responsibility to show why their generation is worse off than any other. For one thing it is probably not true, and besides, there is a bit of Monty Python in all of us and we don't want our generation to be outdone in its perceived hardships!

My purpose in these chapters is not to make value judgements about whether today's teenagers are better or worse off. It is simply to say that there are important differences from other generations, to the extent that it is right and fair to view them as a different cultural group.

Different stages

Not that this is intended, of course, to give the impression that teenagers can be treated as one group. It is blatantly obvious that a boy in Year Nine struggling with early physical changes is very different from the girl in the sixth form whose independence and identity are much more established. Here lies yet another challenge to those working with teenagers. Not only are they a separate cultural group from adults in society, but at different stages they are distinct from each other.

Nevertheless, there are three ways in which I believe teenagers today can be broadly understood to be different:

- in the way they are generally different from adults;
- in the way today's experience of adolescence is very different from the experience of previous generations of teenagers;
- in the way they are the ones most affected by a changing world.

Over the next three chapters we are going to look at each one of these in a little more detail.

6

Life Spent in Front of the Mirror
(How young people are generally different from adults)

Our church culture ... cannot be recreated in the homes of those who use computers, are entertained by videos, dream of pop stars and winning the lottery and whose seaside visits are now prefaced by the word Costa.[1]

Peer pressure

I used to drive a Talbot Samba. One day I was giving three lads a lift home from football when they all dived down behind the front seat. It had the effect of making it look as if I was the only one in the car.

Concerned that they might be in some kind of trouble, I asked the reason for their behaviour, and got a straight answer: 'Those lads back there go to our school and we wouldn't be seen dead in a car like this!' That was it. There was only one thing for it. I reversed down the street, wound down the window and shouted at the gang on the corner, 'Have you seen who I've got in my car?'

If I had accepted the frantic promises coming from

the floor of my Talbot Samba over the next few seconds, I would have inherited the collective wealth of all three families! As I drove off, having spared their blushes after all, you would have thought that I had just saved their lives.

Peer pressure is the social and inner pressure to live up to the expectations of others in order to gain their acceptance and approval. It takes up huge amounts of a teenager's time and emotional energy. Sometimes teenagers try so hard to be in with the rest that they end up pretending to be what they are not and enjoying what they obviously don't.

It is not that adults don't suffer from peer pressure (as every parent knows), but it is the sheer brazenness and intensity of the adolescent peer group that sets them apart. Peers should not be confused with friends (at least as adults understand them). Friends, by most definitions, are accepting and tolerant. In a peer group you are only as good as your last performance. It is an uncomfortable place to be. 'Young people try to get by with a little help from their peers. They form their tribal patterns with their own rituals and codes of behaviour. It doesn't really work, but it is better than nothing.'[2]

Peer groups

Young people, collectively at least, tend to value their independence, keep their distance and remain separate from the adult world of their parents. In doing so, they usually end up forming groups. Groups of teenagers operate around a common image and a common stock of information. Conforming to that image and know-ledge of that information propels group members up or down the pecking order. The image and information can be anything – a label, a band, a team, a sport, a computer – anything that acts as a social glue to the group involved.

Teenage groups often tend to shut out the adult world by keeping their world a very private one. The more it belongs to them, the less it belongs to adults. It is not uncommon for these groups to share values which are frowned upon by the adult world (for example, while parents value hard work, many teenagers value dossing; while adults encourage responsibility, many teenagers will try to avoid it). Often groups of teenagers will seek to shock the adult world, implicitly communicating through their music, fashion and language that they want their space.

The point is, even if teenagers eventually grow up to be not too dissimilar from their parents, most adolescents, at one time or another, want to be seen and understood as very different and often distant from their parents' adult world.

Life spent in front of the mirror

According to the respected educationalist, David Day, teenagers are preoccupied with three basic questions: Do I like myself? Can I manage? Am I an individual? In other words, a preoccupation with themselves and their emerging identity.

Puberty only serves to sharpen this focus. Along with their developing adult bodies comes all the physical and emotional debris of change. Greasy hair, spots, breaking voice or periods would be bad enough at the best of times, but when it is all lived out against a backdrop of our *Baywatch* media culture, it makes life in front of the mirror an uncomfortable one and school showers the ultimate form of torture!

Of course insecurities carry over into adulthood, but the unique physical and emotional changes of adolescence, the insecurities that these create and the

LIFE SPENT IN FRONT OF THE MIRROR ...

thought, time and energy (not to mention money) that they eat up, are a major difference between teenagers and adults. This fundamentally affects the way they perceive themselves and the way they are communicated with.

Language

Another issue which heightens the cultural barrier between young people and adults is the one of language. Most attempts at cross-cultural communication involve overcoming a language barrier, and working with teenagers is no exception.

Any use of language depends on shared meaning of words, and with many of today's teenagers it is simply not there. It is not there because the meaning of words changes over time. 'The ideal of timeless English is sheer nonsense. No living language can be timeless. You might as well ask for a motionless river.'[3] 'In today's world Shakespeare would be a semi-literate.'[4]

This evolving of language is to a major extent driven by young people themselves as they use words to establish their own distinctive group identity. 'Many youth sub-cultures identify words which are keys into the culture. These words act as luggage in which young people pack all their sub-cultural belongings and say this is home.'[5]

So, for example, at the time of writing, in Luton at least, 'cussing' means 'taking the mickey', 'skanking' means 'not turning up', 'sound' means 'all right', 'fish' is an insult, 'bad' means 'good' and 'pukka' means 'excellent'.[6]

This exclusivity of language can cause big problems for the church as our words can unintentionally send the message that young people are not at home with us.

> I have listened to you chatting, preacher,
>   chatting from the heart,
> But didn't dig your message, 'cos you lost me at the start.
> I'm sure you said them from your heart,
>   the things you had to say,
> But heart is not sufficient if your lips get in the way.[7]

Understanding language in working with young people is difficult. For one thing, it is changing so fast; for another, it is regionally based, so a word could mean something in Liverpool and have an entirely different meaning in Luton. Probably the greatest problem, though, is that on the mission field, at least the missionary normally knows when he or she is not being understood. Sadly this is missed by many involved in youth mission today.

YOUR HEART IS NOT SUFFICIENT
IF YOUR LIPS GET IN THE WAY...

Summary of Chapter 6

Just by looking at the very general, obvious differences between teenagers and adults, their different cultural specs are plain to see. But there is much more to young people being understood as a different cultural group than that.

7

You Were Never Their Age

(How today's teenagers' experience of adolescence is different from that of previous generations)

The trouble is that if we leave it there, most adults still instinctively feel that to communicate with this generation is just a question of remembering back to when they were teenagers. We naively talk about a generation gap as if the only difference is the years in

THE GENERATION GAP IS MORE THAN THE YEARS IN BETWEEN...

between. The truth is that even in my generation (and I am only thirty-three) we were not young like they are young today. We were never their age.

You never had that body

'Better diet makes bigger people quite quickly. "The few" would be fewer still today. If the RAF had to put modern pilots into Spitfires and Hurricanes the majority would not be able to fit behind the joy stick!'[1]

Teenagers today are maturing earlier physically. There is evidence to suggest that improvements in environment, diet and medical care have resulted in the onset of puberty reaching girls as young as nine and ten, and boys at ten and eleven. Literally, such individuals become children with adult bodies. This inevitably has significant effects on their behaviour, the way they dress, the sports they play and not least, of course, their sexual experimentation.

You were never that sexy

With adult bodies coming along sooner into a media world that uses sex as its number one attention grabber; into a culture where access to relationships with the opposite sex is more relaxed than at any previous time in recorded history, and moral guidance is almost negligible, is it little wonder that sexual activity is more widespread among younger teenagers than perhaps ever before?

> In 1994, the Sexual behaviour in Britain study found that 10 per cent of women aged between twenty-five and thirty-four had had more than ten sexual partners, compared with 4 per cent of their mothers' generation. About 19 per cent of HIV infections in the UK are among young people aged between fifteen and twenty-four.[2]

The Trust for the Study of Adolescents provides statistical evidence that young people are engaging in sexual activity at an earlier age than ever before – 28 per cent of boys and over 19 per cent of girls having had their first experience of intercourse before their sixteenth birthday.[3]

You were never so old so young

> 'We are finally learning, though with some regret, that all the problems and issues that filled high school programming a decade ago, must now become the subject of junior high programmes and 10-13 year olds.'[4]

With physical maturity arriving earlier; with our information society making young people more broadly aware of the world than ever before; with earlier sexual encounters; with our education system giving important decisions to teenagers as young as thirteen; with large amounts of unsupervised free time and many finding part-time work – it is little wonder that social commentators refer to the 'erosion of childhood'. The pressure is on to grow up quicker, and what the consequences of this early exposure to the adult world will be are not yet clear, but one thing is for sure: people get 'older' younger these days.

You were never so young for so long

Here lies an interesting fault line in our cultural experience. On the one hand, parents encourage the more rapid passing of childhood because, in so many ways, more adult behaviour makes their parental role easier. On the other hand, with a general atmosphere of uncertainty, people fight shy of commitment and the responsibility traditionally associated with adult life. At the same time, governments encourage further education and the marketing world continues to hold out the young, free and single lifestyle as the most fulfilling. The net result? The price our post-modern world pays? An adolescence which starts earlier and finishes later than it ever did before.

You were never that influential

This in turn gives teenagers influence. A market that grows at both ends means that more resources are spent on gaining its attention, and when the combined forces of the fashion and music industries, the computer and literary world and the leisure conglomerates, to name but a few, bombard the market place with adolescent-friendly images and products, it begins to shape and change the nature of society itself.

Respectable adult fashion houses upgrade the chic boutique styles, mainstream musicians add a subtle house beat to make their music more youth friendly and, lo and behold, we all want to be young again!

You never changed so fast

Here lies one of the forces of constant change in the music and fashion industries. Teenagers see themselves as different from adults and, what is more, want to be seen as different. So when adult culture mimics adolescent trends, it is time for the young to move on. This makes the teenage market a turbulent and fickle one. 'If it is in, you can be sure it is on its way out!' It is a world that is constantly reinventing itself – a constantly moving target. All in all, it is a gift for the advertisers, as they always have a new product to sell!

ADULT CULTURE MIMICS ADOLESCENT TRENDS...

You never had so many choices

This in turn has led to a fragmenting of adolescent culture. Again, driven by the ad men's need to sell and the teenage desire to make a distinctive statement, the once clear delineation that you were either a Mod or a Rocker(!) then became a much more confusing array of choices.

For a few years it seemed the teenage market would just continue to diversify, but now there is evidence that a stronger middle ground is again emerging. Rather than having more specific 'tribal' identities we now have the indistinct mass of multinational sports label clones. Perhaps in current fashion we have another example of the 'option paralysis' of our post-modern world. When faced with so many choices we fail to make any distinctive choices at all.

You were never that troubled

There can be little doubt that today's teenagers do live with the consequences of a society which has lost direction. A major study by William K. Kay and Leslie J. Francis looked at a wide range of aspects of young people's lives. The survey covered more than 13,000 pupils at state schools in England and Wales in Years Nine and Ten (thirteen- and fourteen-year-olds).

In response to the negative statement 'I have some-times considered taking my own life', 24 per cent of boys and 30 per cent of girls questioned in the survey agreed, even though the official figures for suicides in the whole ten to nineteen age group are much lower. Some 60 per cent of girls and 45 per cent of boys admitted to often feeling depressed and only just over half (54 per cent of boys and 57 per cent of girls) could agree to 'My life has a sense of purpose'.

The statistics go on:

- In 1990 there were 2,910 permanent exclusions from school. In 1995 there were 12,458.[5]
- Two thirds of teenagers think it likely that they will be mugged or beaten up.[6]
- One third think that there is a high chance of them being sexually assaulted.[6]
- 25 per cent of fifteen- to sixteen-year-olds have tried cannabis.[7]
- 20 per cent of nine- to fifteen-year-olds had their first alcoholic drink by the age of eight.[8]
- 1 million young people between sixteen and twenty-five were out of work in 1994. Some 88,000 school leavers were unemployed in the same year.[9]
- In London in 1994 the unemployment rate for black males between the ages of sixteen and twenty-four was 62 per cent.
- Two thirds of thirteen- to fifteen-year-olds are not sure any more what is right or wrong.[10]
- The third highest killer of adolescents is suicide.

As far as teenage crime is concerned, the picture is far from encouraging. 'Every known factor associated with teenage crime is escalating. Unless we address the issues, our prospects as a peaceful country are terrible beyond measure.'[11]

One cannot help being reminded of Schlossberg's famous quote: 'A society that cannot tolerate a judge beyond history, will find that it can tolerate anything else.'

You were never that preoccupied

Life spent in front of the mirror can also have its more serious consequences. Peter Wilson argues that when a teenager's natural preoccupation with self meets the cultural changes of fragmenting families, a lack of moral absolutes and the increasingly illusionary world of the electronic media, it turns into narcissism.[12] He defines narcissism as an inward preoccupation with self, which leads to social indifference and selfish insistence at the expense of others.

It is not that adults are not self-focused, of course, but during periods of adolescence at least, self can almost uncontrollably intrude upon everything.

This kind of attitude was vividly demonstrated by a national opinion poll survey for the BBC in 1993. One in eight teenagers said that they would commit violent crime and one in three said that they would commit credit card fraud if they were sure to get away with it.

Summary of Chapter 7

There is much more to the generation gap than the years in between. Today's experience of adolescence is very different from my generation's. I was never fourteen like they are fourteen and it stands to reason that their cultural specs will inevitably be different from mine.

8

Post-Modern Puppets

(How today's teenagers are most influenced by a changing world)

> Every few hundred years throughout western history, a sharp transformation has occurred. In a matter of decades, society altogether rearranges itself.... Fifty years later, a new world exists and the people born into that world cannot even imagine the world in which their grandparents lived.... Our age is such a period of transformation.[1]

Human nature has not suddenly changed at the end of the twentieth century. The joys and tensions of adolescence are still basically the same. What has clearly changed, however, is the environment in which these teenage years are now lived out. With a very different kind of culture surrounding them, there is evidence to suggest that today's teenagers will grow up with a set of cultural specs different from our own.

So let us take a brief look at the changing world today's teenagers live in. First, though, it is important to recognise that many of the issues I raise here do not affect teenagers alone. To some extent or other they affect all generations of people in twentieth-century Britain. My point, though, is that teenagers are *more* influenced by them. While the winds of change may buffet older generations, the younger generation can be swept off their feet. To put it another way, when the dust settles after cultural change, it is just another layer for adults who have lived through change before. For young people growing up, though, it is the very soil in which their roots are placed. It shapes and determines who they are to become. In short, living in today's climate has more effect on young people's cultural specs than it does on ours.

Cultural backdrop

A GENERATION WITH PMT

PMT stands for pre-millennial tension (of course!). Adolescence today is acted out against a unique historical backdrop, a defining moment in world history – the dawning of a new millennium. Today's teenagers will be only the second generation in the history of the planet to welcome one in. Some commentators are of the view, though, that as we approach the year 2000, there will be a growing realisation that not only are they the second generation, but they may well also be the last. The world, they say, is unlikely to make it to a third millennium.

> Look at the budget. We are borrowing a billion dollars every twenty-four hours and in the process endangering the future for our children, yet nobody is doing anything about it. Why not? Because genuine political dialogue has been almost completely replaced by high stakes competition for the ever shorter attention span of the electorate. The future whispers while the present shouts. Somehow, we have convinced ourselves that we care far less about what happens to our children than about avoiding the inconvenience and discomfort of paying our

own bills. So instead of accepting responsibility for our choices, we simply dump huge mountains of both debt and pollution on future generations.[2]

THE FUTURE WHISPERS WHILST THE PRESENT SHOUTS...

'Capitalism has led to the throwing out of the principle of housekeeping and fair distribution. Exponential growth is the basic law of economics, within no limits. It is growth for growth's sake. There is no overarching purpose. A minority is urged to multiply its wants. The majority lacks basic needs of existence and the whole economic system is threatened. If it was in a human body, they would call it cancer.'[3]

In short, today's teenager grows up in a world of PMTs – a backdrop that we are possibly without a potential future.

BRITISH INSTITUTIONAL LIFE

Britain's teenagers are growing up with the foundations of British society creaking and groaning at the end of the twentieth century. As the BBC's John Simpson noted in his end of year review in 1995, each of Britain's four main institutions had had a bad year. Parliament was seen to be losing power to Brussels, our legal system had been shown to have failed in a number of high profile appeal court cases, the monarchy was increasingly seen in a bad light and the Church of England was divided within itself on major issues.

Now I don't think for one moment that the average teenager is remotely bothered with what John Simpson says, but my point is this: 'We are an administered society from our identity wristband at birth to our death certificate. We are characterised by a thick network of regulatory institutions.'[4] If those institutions are seen to be crumbling, felt to be under-funded and under-staffed and unable to do the job, it shapes the atmosphere of the society in which we grow up. This in turn defines the way we think about our country and our role in society, crafting our cultural specs in the process.

Cultural foundations

HAPPY FAMILIES?

Today's teenagers are living through a period of history when society is in danger of losing its family structure. Fourteen per cent, or one in seven families with children, are lone-parent families today. Since 1980 there have been 1.8 million divorces. Disruption to the family (which after all is the foundational anchor of any society) has far-reaching consequences. Many children are left without any model of a lasting committed relationship between adults and their trust in people is damaged by parents who are perceived to have walked out on them.

> Divorce is associated with more adverse outcomes for children than the death of a parent, and the remarriage of a parent appears in some circumstances to add to the children's difficulties. Our findings are supported by a very large body of research of many different kinds.[5]

In a society where the ambiguous phrase 'current partner' is the preferred option for the person we live with; where 'maintenance agreements' and 'access arrangements' are part of mainstream life; when Sunday mornings see the country's parks full of children with their Sunday fathers; when everyone from teachers to politicians, from mortgage lenders to churchmen are trying to come to terms with the changing definition of family, it is little wonder that there is confusion. For families still together, things have also changed. It is not much easier for the latchkey generation who let themselves in to heat up their tea as their parents work shifts, or for the 'absence makes the heart go purchasing' crowd whose earning parents make up for a lack of time with an abundance of presents.

'WE DON'T NEED NO EDUCATION'

Few experiences are more important in shaping our cultural specs than that of our formal education – not simply in what we learn, but also in how we learn it. Over recent years in Britain, education has changed a great deal.

What children are taught has ebbed and flowed with educational trends. In History, for example, a focus on dates and facts gave way to interpretation and appreciation of the bigger picture, only to be pointed firmly back to the dates and facts by the politicians! Religious Education was exclusively Christian, then multi-faith and now supposedly 'predominantly Christian'. In English, spelling and grammar have been at times more or less important, and the debate continues about whether continual assessment or exam performance is the best evaluator of a student's achievement.

The changing face of education

Gone are the days of:

- 11-Plus
- O-levels and CSEs
- Old-fashioned apprenticeships
- The oldest son goes to college
- Only the rich kids go to college
- Leaving school at fourteen
- Leaving school with no qualifications leads to a lifetime of shelf-filling

Now we have:

- GCSEs
- AS levels
- Modularised A-levels
- GNVQs
- NVQs
- BTECs
- HNDs
- Modern apprenticeships.

However, it is in the way things are taught that the most important changes have occurred and these have far-reaching consequences for shaping a child's worldview.

Didactic versus critical

In recent years there has been a steady move towards a more relative or critical understanding in education as the power of rationalism has declined in the Western world. Facts are no longer given to be recorded and then at a later date regurgitated. That old style didactic model is avoided wherever possible now. In fact, the world of indisputable facts has become decidedly smaller. In today's classroom, facts are only someone's views – opinions to be questioned, uncovered, prodded a little, compared with others and then evaluated. Critical education is in, and with it, critical specs.

School management

Behind the scenes the management of schools has also changed dramatically. LMS, school league tables, national curriculum, under-funding and under-staffing – you name it, it has happened. The net result has been a considerable shift in the way school is perceived by young people. For example, fewer and fewer teachers are running the extra-curricula activities these days because there are simply too many other burdens placed upon them for them to think about gym club and hockey as well. In many sixth forms, cost-effective management has meant staggered lunch breaks in order to utilise classroom space for the maximum number of students. Almost all lunchtime clubs have disappeared and with them a sense of community. ID cards are worn to convince uniformed security men of your right to attend college, and free periods require a trip into town as there are not even enough spaces in the library to house everyone. It can be argued that the current administration of our education system, far from encouraging responsibility and citizenship, is actually shaping a generation who see themselves as the client and the state as their impersonal provider.

Discipline

Schools blame parents and parents blame schools, but irrespective of blame, school discipline is seen to be breaking down. Exclusions are at an all-time high, and parent boycotts and staff industrial action are regularly in the news. Teaching morale is, according to experienced teachers, at an all-time low.

Today a huge amount of time is spent during teacher training on 'classroom management' – discipline to you and me. One cannot help feeling, though, that all the techniques of control in the world are a bit like the Emperor's new clothes: ultimately there is nothing there. Society has taken away the right of adults to tell children what to do, and what is worse, this generation knows it! What the long-term implications are for this we can but speculate. All we know is that every day of education fashions the cultural specs of today's teenagers.

Cultural experience

TOTAL MEDIA EXPOSURE

Today's media world is intrusive. Every waking moment it competes for our attention through one form or another. Teenagers are especially vulnerable to such bombardment.

The heavy bit

'The various forms of media are the icons of our society. Through them we see what we want to value and esteem, by them we make choices. In the matrix of our experience and what we watch or listen to, our views and values are shaped. Then in turn it is with those opinions and values that we perceive, interpret and discern our world, our context.'[6]

Advertising

Advertising might not be new, but its intrusion into our daily lives is immeasurable. Radio, TV, magazines, papers, bill boards, flyers – it is so much part of everyday life that we don't notice it, or at least we don't think we do! The tactics of the ad-man become ever more sophisticated. Huge budgets make an unscrupulous play upon human emotions and frailties. Gillette (the best a man can get?!) have got such imagery down to a fine art form. It is highly irrational, while paradoxically being highly effective.

'In the fifth century, Simeon Stylites spent thirty-five years starving himself at the top of a pole, testifying to the power of God. Today's woman spends more than thirty-five years starving herself to look like a pole, testifying to the power of advertising.'[7]

Today's teenagers are to be forgiven if they assume that they were born to shop or that happiness equals consumption. It is working, though. The youth market in the United States alone is worth $78 billion a year![8]

'Modern ad men have gone one stage beyond and now talk of synergy as they seek to produce a film with a best selling sound track that generates a video with clips from the film that helps sell the album which is promoted on MTV. This is precisely how the film *The*

Bodyguard was developed, as the central core of a multimedia extravaganza which netted over 80 million dollars. "Malls are the cathedrals of late modernity, where people come to gaze and wonder in the sacred space, to offer homage and pay their dues to the gods of mammon."[9]

HAPPINESS = CONSUMPTION

Magazines

Teenage magazines are a huge and lucrative market for which big business competes. What will sell becomes the be all and end all, so teenage magazines tend to slump to the lowest common denominator. Outside of the special interest titles, what is important is the overall image and impression of the magazine's design, the fashion pages, the media star gossip and, of course, lots and lots of sex. In other words, designed to please at the shallowest of levels. 'Watch a teenage girl going through her favourite magazine, she is comparing herself to images, imagining herself with certain products displayed, comparing male portraits to her own fantasies, and in general being instructed as to how she can better live her life socially. In effect, she is having her cultural quiet time.'[10]

Television

'The average teenager watches 28 hours of TV a week and the average working person 18 hours a week. By the time you are 60 you have spent 9 years in front of the television. That changes the way we see the world.'[11]

Part of the problem is that young people are not a critical audience of the media. They struggle to distinguish between the projected image and the underlying message.

When the head of MTV, Ben Johnson, was interviewed by Tony Campolo, he was asked, 'How do you seek to influence teenagers?' His reply was stark: 'We don't seek to influence them, we own them.' He went on to say that what appeals to kids is a diet of anger and intimacy.[12]

Several commentators have made the point that the

nature of story has changed in our TV culture. Parents used to tell stories to children and those stories were imbibed with their own values and worldviews. Today's parents, though, often take the easy option and delegate story-telling to the television, without ever really thinking through the values and motives that the TV programme-makers have.

With increasing evidence that the nine o'clock watershed means nothing for a generation who have a TV in their bedrooms, the debate staggers on about how TV shapes the way we behave. Surely even in these confused times we are able to see this one clearly. If what we watch on TV does not influence, at least in part, the way we behave, then why do we spend billions of pounds every year on TV advertising?

It is not only the content of programmes, though, that is of concern. It is also the nature of the communication itself. Some have argued that what teenagers gain in visual sophistication, they lose in their ability to communicate. Others would see exposure to TV actually undermining the nature of reality itself.

> To go straight from Bosnia to One Foot in the Grave, to be treated as having a two-minute attention span, to be assumed to need more and more stimulation by increasingly startling presentations, to be bombarded by a succession of instantaneous experiences, to be endlessly diverted, to have no time to pause and reflect, is to have everything reduced to the same level of significance – or insignificance.[13]

The task of any parent in today's media world must be to try to teach their children that watching TV is a cultural exercise and must be done selectively, for every day it shapes the way that we perceive reality.

HIGH-TECH SOCIETY

The technological revolution is changing life as we know it, and it is those who grow up in this Internet culture who are shaped the most by its possibilities. So, for example, today's generation view time and space differently from any previous generation. During World War Two, my parents heard and read of news from the Front perhaps a few days after it had occurred. My generation viewed events in the Falklands War only a matter of hours after they had happened. Today's generation saw live scenes from the Gulf War at precisely the same moment as the military generals, such are the improvements in satellite technology. Such access makes the world seem smaller, the seeming giants of time and space now made dwarfs by the creation of the microchip. Technology enables this generation to think bigger and faster than any generation before it.

> Over the past twenty years, there has been the equivalent to a million-fold improvement in computing power. Thus, a task that took one year to complete twenty years ago, would take merely thirty seconds to complete today. At Microsoft, we anticipate that there will be another million-fold increase in computing power over the next twenty years.[14]

Technology also changes our perception of authority. Previous generations tended to assume that behind the scenes national leaders had access to more information than the public, so tended to trust them more. Today's generation knows that the information playing field is almost level these days and it is much more likely to question leaders' judgement as a result.

Cultural values

IT'S MY CHOICE

Today everybody wants to be free and that freedom is measured by having choices. What we choose, it seems, is not as important as actually having the freedom to choose in the first place! Choice is now a value in itself, a state of mind, a priority. The consequences are that obligation melts to option, fact to fashion. An increase in choice and change leads to a decrease in commitment and continuity. Choices are seen like a Kleenex tissue, not like a silk hankie. They are disposable, so marriages, beliefs, homes, all are commitment shy convictions.[15]

Freedom, though, is not about having choices. Freedom is making the right choices. Once again, however, it is young people who pay a heavy price when society gets this wrong.

It is little wonder that in this bewildering world of choice, many young people behave in a way that in effect limits their choices. It makes life less confusing.

Cultural beliefs

The title 'post-modern' says it all. We are a post-modern society. In other words, we know what we have come from, but we have little idea as to where we are going. Like a bad politician, we define ourselves by saying what we are not! We are a society in transition.

Hardly surprising, then, that when it comes to beliefs many today feel like they are on a journey, reluctantly accepting that humanity cannot solve the problems of the world and tentatively open to an increased belief in the supernatural. Society is less sure of itself these days.

The heavy bit

'People no longer trust the Enlightenment answers, they do not expect reason to explain the deeper mysteries the Millennium makes them think about.'[16]

Such views are reflected in the statistical analysis of teenage beliefs by Dr Leslie Francis. He surveyed successive generations of pupils in two comprehensive schools for their attitudes to Christianity in 1974, 1978, 1982, 1986 and 1990. There was a progressive hardening of student attitudes until 1990, when students began to be more positive and indicated an openness to religious issues. This was, however, an openness to the possibility of a religious dimension, not to a commitment to religious practice.[17]

IT WORKS, DOESN'T IT?

Given this sense of general uncertainty, people tend to try and find what works for them. In fact, this pragmatism could be defined as the most commonly held belief in Britain today.

It used to be said, 'It is true, therefore it works.' It was then said, 'It works, therefore it is true.' Now it's, 'It works, and that is all there is to it!'

So in the market place of belief, people shop around for the best bargains on offer, and today's teenagers are growing up in a DIY society. It is a pick and mix arrangement where bits of, say, popular psychology are blended with traditional Christianity, layered on a base of secularism and given a touch of Eastern mysticism for added spice!

This pragmatic approach, however, is a bit like a Little Chef restaurant. It's an OK place to rest on the journey, but not somewhere you would choose to live. A pragmatic lifestyle might be valid for a time, while trying to find truth, but to stay there for ever, resigned to never finding the meaning to life, is a despairing and empty place to be. 'Pragmatism is the last stand of a culture which has lost its true centre.'[18]

Where does this leave us?

One of the best definitions that I have come across of our world today is written by Dave Tomlinson:

The post-modern world is a world which understands itself through biological rather than mechanistic models; a world where people see themselves as belonging to the environment rather than over it or apart from it. A world distrustful of institutions, hierarchies, centralised bureau-cracies and male dominated organisations. It is a world in which networks and local grass root activities take precedence over large scale structures and grand designs; a world in which the book age is giving way to the screen age; a world hungry for spirituality yet dismissive of systematised religion. It is a world in which image and reality are so deeply intertwined that it is difficult to draw the line between the two.[19]

Life in the present tense

Post-modernism is life in the present tense. Uprooted from our past, unclear about our future – the now is all-important. Choices are made on the basis of what meaning and satisfaction they bring today.

Zygmunt Baumen describes us as vagabonds.[20] Nomads have purpose, pilgrims have a destination, but disillusionment with the present is all that drives the vagabond on.

There is at least one ray of light, though. While there is little doubt that our post-modern Western society is heading in the opposite direction to the world the Bible writers envisaged, it could be said that it is at the same time becoming more like the world in which the New Testament was originally written. Then as now, Christianity had to compete in the market place of belief. Perhaps more so now than for many years there is a more direct application of the methods of the early church to our situation today.

Summary of Section Two

Given all that we have read over the last three chapters, it is little wonder that the Anglican Church, in its report 'Youth Apart', drew the following conclusion: 'The primary frontier which needs to be crossed in mission to young people is not so much a generation gap, as a profound change in the overall culture.'

Here lies the heart of this book. This is what motivates me to write.

It is legitimate to say that young people today can be a different cultural group. That means the church of Jesus Christ has things to challenge in youth culture if it is to be faithful to the gospel. *Critically, though, it also has things to learn from young people.* At the moment, this rarely, if ever, happens, and both the church and young people are more impoverished as a result.

The rest of this book goes on to outline some of the lessons the church can learn by taking young people seriously, and to explore how the church can be led out of its culture trap by working with and listening to today's teenagers.

I am reminded of David Pawson speaking on the story of Samson. The once mighty judge of Israel was now an impotent, stumbling shadow of his former self. At last trusting in God alone, he asked a young boy to guide him to the centre of the Philistine temple, and in one final incredible display of strength, God's enemies were defeated. Possibly God will do it again, Pawson ventured. This time the slumbering giant of the church, stripped of every security save its faith in God, will be brought to the centre of our nation's life to display his power, and perhaps again he will use young people to do it.

SECTION THREE

Essential Youth

Introduction

After ten years in youth ministry, I have yet to face a problem in the youth programme which does not have a parallel in the history of the wider church. For a variety of reasons though (to do with size, lack of tradition and the flexibility of the people involved), the problems are easier to address in the youth ministry context.

Here lies the heart of this final section. Leadership strategies that work in the more simplified atmosphere of the youth group have something to teach the wider church. If it is good practice in the youth group, the principle will apply to the adult congregation too.

So what can we learn?

9

Evangelistic Essentials

The church that turns in on itself is no longer a church.'[1]

We saw in Chapter 2 that the basic problem with evangelism today is twofold:

1. We are failing to take seriously the cultural setting of the people we are trying to reach.
2. In trying to reach them, we are encumbered by a church culture which is out of tune with the rest of society.

Let us see how working with young people helps the church in its evangelistic task.

'To evangelise is to proclaim God's good news about Jesus Christ, to the end that people will believe in him, find life in him and ultimately be conformed to his image, not ours.'[2]

The story behind the headlines

I was once asked to act as a youth consultant for a church. From the outside, everything looked fine. It was larger than average, it had a good number of young families and it had an effective and efficient leadership team. The problem was the young people – at least that's what they said. They were just not there! They attended the mid-week clubs, but despite several attempts to encourage them they would not stay to the services.

I met with the minister and then separately with all the other leaders involved so that they could tell me what they really felt the problems were. Needless to say, all of them had their own theories and their own angle on things! The youth leaders were clear that the services were too long and boring, and that the teaching and music style failed to engage with adolescents, while one of the elders confided in me that if only there was better Bible teaching and less entertainment in the youth programme, the problems with young people would not exist in the first place!

Finally, the night arrived when I met with them all together. Everybody in the room was focused on the problem with young people. I was about to disappoint them.

I began with a question: 'When was the last time you saw an adult converted from a non-Christian background?' Everybody looked a bit puzzled – after all, we were here to talk about teenagers! After some discussion, it was finally agreed that they could only remember one man, and he had come to faith a few years previously. An embarrassed silence fell upon the room as the truth began to sink in. I put up an OHP slide: 'This church does not have a problem with young people. Fundamentally, this church has a problem with the gospel!'

As any counsellor will tell you, the first problem that people start talking about is rarely the real issue. The presenting problem is often little more than a doorway to the root issue itself. So it is with young people in the church. They are often the presenting problem, but rarely the root of the problem. Young people are a sensitive thermometer to an ice aged church, however much youth leaders might try to warm things up. They are often the first to feel the chill of cultural irrelevance; the first to feel left out in the cold by a church obsessed with looking inwards. So they leave – on a national scale in their droves. But when they do, it is a symptom of the cancer in church life, not the tumour itself. Fundamentally, the church today does not have a problem with young people. It has a problem with the gospel.

Think about it logically. Teenagers are in all likelihood the single largest group of non-Christians who regularly attend your church activities. For a church whose faithfulness to God is at least in part measured by its attempts to reach the lost, doesn't that make what they think and like important?

If we approach youth work from this perspective, what else is there to learn about the church's evangelistic task?

Cultural captives

Working with young people quickly exposes the church's cultural blind spots.

Every Sunday it happens up and down the country:

teenagers behaving inappropriately in church. It becomes almost a ritual as both sides take it as far as they can without actually disrupting the services. On the one hand, teenagers might talk, fidget, pass round sweets, go to the toilet, giggle, even fight, but normally to a level that lets everyone know they are there, rather than cause an outright interruption to proceedings. On the other side, the valiant youth leaders glare, have quiet words during hymns, bribe, prod, and move next to the young people concerned, again while not actually halting proceedings with an outright confrontation. In its simplest terms, it is a game of dare and brinkmanship!

IN SIMPLEST TERMS IT'S A GAME
OF DARE AND BRINKMANSHIP...

I have played for both sides more times than I care to remember, but now I have come to see that when teenagers' attitude and behaviour are seen as inappropriate for church life, it is often more because the way we do church is inappropriate for today's world. Of course, I am not wanting to condone bad behaviour, but unless we are able to see what it highlights in church practice, we are missing what I believe is a God-given opportunity. Much of what we do is boring, many of our practices are outdated, many of our methods have not worked, so why are we so resistant to change? If the only reason is that we are comfortable this way, the sacrifices demanded by the cross of Christ have been bypassed somewhere along the line.

Here lies one of the reasons why young people are essential to the church in its evangelistic task. They are a constant reminder that we must be relevant to contemporary society. They are sometimes a God-given thorn in our flesh to teach us that personal preference is not the issue. It is what communicates with the lost that counts.

To dismiss teenagers as loud and abrasive is to miss the fact that the whole of our culture is more and more youth orientated and wrongly assumes that because visiting adults don't complain, they find patterns of church appealing and engaging. If that is so, why are they such infrequent attenders?

The uncomfortable truth that the church has to face up to is that however unfair, selfish and mistaken some teenagers' comments about church life are, they are nevertheless hitting a raw nerve. At the end of the twentieth century, God's people are missing engaging with the world by a very big margin indeed.

Every church struggles to find a service appropriate for everyone. I am not for a moment wanting to suggest that all services should be youth orientated.

Such a move would not only unnecessarily alienate many others in society, but it would sell teenagers themselves short, as they too must learn of the personal sacrifices we must all make for the sake of the gospel. If it is not modelled to them by older Christians in church, how will they learn?

When we get to know them and spend time with them, we are given an insight into teenagers' immediate and emotional world. It is throbbing with energy and life. Many a time I have sat in church with them and thought, 'If I am honest, *I* am bored. No wonder they are struggling!' Yet in other contexts, I have been privileged to hear them pray and ask penetrating questions about what the gospel means today, and demonstrate great courage in their faith, all of which reveals a genuine relationship with God. It is at these moments that the cultural captivity of the church becomes clear. There has to be more attractive and engaging ways of doing church for people today.

'92% of young people don't come to church because they don't want to. Church is so alien in its dress, language, layout, music, rituals, structure of authority, sexism.'[3]

The real enemy

It was going really well. I had been invited into a local school to answer questions about my faith. The Year Eleven class had prepared some good questions and we had had some fun as we negotiated the usual apologetics issues. As the end of the lesson approached, though, questions became more personal and honest. It was obvious that a number in the class were genuinely searching. It was a marvellous opportunity as people were prepared to be vulnerable about what was missing in their life.

All too soon the bell went, but as the kids started to pack away their books, I still felt excited about the potential of our time together. I was quickly brought back to reality as the teacher closed the lesson. 'Our thanks to Mr Hickford this morning. As you know, this is the start of our series "What my faith means to me". Next week we have the imam from Bury Park Mosque visiting and the following week we have the rabbi from the synagogue. Your homework for this week is to prepare another set of good questions for the imam. You may go.' As the class trooped out, now thinking about what they were going to have for lunch, the words of Steve Turner came to mind:

> Today we don't stone prophets,
> we don't even censor them,
> we don't put them in prison,
> we just put them in perspective.[4]

When I was at school, there was only one faith that I knew anything about. We sang Christian hymns in assembly and despite it being a large, modern comprehensive, we studied Christianity in RE. Awareness and appreciation of people of other beliefs came in social studies, but the thought that what they believed might be of some help to me was never even hinted at. It never entered into my thinking that their faith could be an option for me, or even that it could possibly be true.

Today's multiple choice world is very different. A

multi-cultural society demands multi-faith education. Our media world's fascination for the weird and the wonderful helps to ensure that we are exposed to an ever increasing and confusing array of gurus, sects, cults and a whole variety of religious teaching.

'I have travelled the world, searching for something in which to believe. My spiritual journey has involved working with Californian New Age teachers, studying with the Indian and Tibetan Holy women and men, being healed by native American Shamans, trance dancing to African drums, visiting sacred Celtic sites, delving into my Jewish roots, studying the power of Kundalini energy and sacred Tantric lovemaking, learning the power of silence, and going inward and celebrating the return of the goddess through connection with Mother Earth... I am currently practising Raj yoga meditation, with the Brarahma Kamaris, an international spiritual organisation founded in India ... I have come a long way from the ad fab days, but I'm just a woman on her own journey to her truth.'[5]

This class had genuine and searching questions, but over three weeks they were about to hear three completely different sets of answers. How could they possibly be expected to weigh them up and decide what was true? I thought about it more as I drove home in the car. They had heard me talk about my personal faith, but that is all it was to them – my personal faith. The thought that it might ultimately be true and have huge implications for them was not likely even to enter their minds.

I believe that there are several things to be learned here by the wider church.

First, evangelism today has to recognise the competition of the market place. Christianity is but one of a number of options on offer from which people can choose what to believe, so the gospel needs to be compared and contrasted to some of the other faiths available.

Such a view gains support from the research that advertising agencies have done into teenage marketing trends. In the now famous Spoilt Brats survey, of Gold, Greenlees and Trott Advertising Agency, it was argued that teenagers, especially today, needed to be sold to differently. These 'divorgenics' have been hurt by their families and are therefore more cautious and untrusting. Their attitudes to people are reflected in their attitudes to products. They look for a strong argument and competitive comparisons, and we must, they suggested, be careful not to insult their intelligence.

In our evangelism, we must also recognise the atmosphere which the sheer number of choices available creates. That these young people had choices about faith was not the problem. After all, if Christianity is true then it can stand up to the toughest competition. The truly awful thing about our society right now is the way that the sheer number of choices erodes our confidence that any of the choices on offer might actually be true. *The real enemy we face is not pluralism. The real enemy is relativism.* There is no longer a confidence in a public truth which is so universal and demonstrable that it applies to everyone. Truth today is what is true for you – an issue of sincerity, not of clarity.

As Clive Calver has written, 'Truth has been lowered

THE NUMBER OF OPTIONS FOR TRUTH HAS ERODED OUR CONFIDENCE IN ANY REAL TRUTH BEING LEFT...

to the level of what can be attained, rather than to the height of what we must aspire to. Contemporary society has moved one step away from the Garden of Eden. No longer do we reject God's truth, we now deny that it even existed.'[6]

Such a dominant atmosphere requires the church to hold a very delicate balance in its proclamation of the gospel if it is to engage genuinely yet faithfully with our world. On the one hand we worship a God who, the Bible tells us, delights in the truth and personifies and epitomises truth itself. On numerous occasions Jesus said, 'I tell you the truth,' and in John 14:6 he claimed to be the one true channel through which people can be reconciled to God. Christians, then, have no option but to believe in universal, absolute and eternal truths to which one day every knee must bow and every tongue confess. A belief in stark contrast to the prevailing atmosphere of a post-modern Western world.

There can be no compromise here. If the church gives up on Jesus' claim to be the exclusive truth, then we have nothing left to offer. Instead we must be robust in showing the damage that the loss of truth brings to society and forever refuse to be packaged into the world of private truths only. We must speak out boldly and wisely – in the political arena, in ethical debates and in shaping the future direction of society.

'The loss of truth is absolutely fundamental. Everything flows from that. You reach the point where we are today as Nietzsche predicted, denying that anything can be affirmed as absolutely true. The only way to tackle a society that has jettisoned absolute truth is to tell the whole story and to tell it with confidence ... for if there is no truth we are just adrift in a shoreless ocean.'[7]

On the other hand, we must remember that every culture has something of God's thumbprint inherent in it and post-modernism is no exception. While we must stand against the loss of truth in society, we must also allow something of the evasiveness of truth, of which today's world is so aware, to bring fresh insight into biblical teaching. Evangelicals, for example, are beginning to realise that our claims to know absolute truths do not hold water in today's world. Post-modernism has helped to remind us that knowing absolute truth now is not a biblical doctrine. Truth is transcendent as he lies beyond us. Truth resides in God, and his ways are greater than ours.

So the great challenge facing the church is to proclaim boldly in the public arena the truth of the gospel with its many implications for society, but with a humility and honest vulnerability which engages a searching world in genuine dialogue.

Truth is stranger than it used to be. Post-modern understanding points us to exciting dimensions of the biblical text of which we were previously unaware.[8]

People, not propositions

Martin appeared to have it all. At sixteen he was head boy, first team football captain, solid academically and had the kind of looks which ensured almost constant female attention.

He was part of a crowd which began to attend a bar we ran and his natural confidence and social skills meant that we got to know each other quite quickly. It soon became apparent, though, that Martin was a pretty shrewd character. He somehow managed to make everyone feel a valued friend without letting them get close.

As the months passed and we prayed about this group of young people, the issue seemed to be how to move beyond the happy but superficial relationships. The key to that was Martin. Gradually, over a two-year period, trust deepened, conversations about faith took place naturally and we made a point of being as open and honest about our relationships with Christ as we could be.

Eventually, after one meeting, Martin cornered me in a manner much more blunt and direct than usual: 'What would you do if I could disprove Christianity to you?' he asked.

'I would resign,' I said, without really thinking.

'In that case, pray with me. I want to become a Christian,' he replied.

Another insight which working with young people like Martin gives to the church about how to reach the modern world is the way that truth is arrived at today. Nothing distinguishes better the difference between the modern and post-modern world than their approaches to what is called epistemology, or theories of how truth is established. 'It is not about differences of opinion, but a fundamental difference in the way that opinion is reached.'[9] Understanding that is fundamental to understanding evangelism in today's world.

The church is basically modernist in its understanding. We proclaim the truth of God's word and expect people to respond. Non-Christians, however, think differently. Martin was typically post-modern in his conversion experience. Truth, for Martin, was relational and experiential before it was propositional. In other words, he arrived at his decision over a long period of time, and it was through the dynamic of interacting with a group of Christians and trying Christianity out on the quiet, rather than being preached a message to which he responded. Objective truth was the last piece of the jigsaw for Martin, not the first.

Here is another doorway to the non-Christian world at large which working with young people provides. As we have already seen, those in a society which has lost its grasp of truth are only left with trying to find out what will work for them. They are not interested in claims to know truth; they are looking around for what works and they are fundamentally looking for it in the people around them.

Once again, this post-modern view brings to light elements of biblical teaching which have sometimes been overlooked. It once again reminds us that our first calling is to follow Christ – to live out something radically different. Rather than simply preach the message we must first live it.

The world judges Christianity not on apologetics, but on the church.

Wider evidence that this kind of approach is working today is to be found in the now-famous Alpha course. Replicated in tens of thousands of churches up and down the country in various denominational settings, Alpha encourages open dialogue alongside relationship building and an understanding that we are all on a spiritual journey together. There is even a willingness to include non-Christians in joint leadership of the groups. It is these principles which go right to the heart of equipping the church for evangelism in today's world.

If this is true it has huge implications for the way individual Christians live their lives. In today's world it is simply not good enough for us to give priority to church activities and pray for people to become Christians. God wants to use us to answer our own prayers. Unless we are giving priority to quality time with non-Christians, how will they ever hear and see the gospel? To pray for revival without making every effort to form genuine friendships with non-Christians is pure escapism!

Sadly, we are very slow to learn. In 1969, Gavin Reid wrote: 'As fishers of men we can no longer wait for the arrival of shoals in carefully built reservoirs and yet we still tie up our people in activities.'[10]

From sex to salvation

Talking to fifteen-year-olds about a Christian view of sex is always a challenging prospect. These days one can't help feeling that it is trying to shut the stable door after the horse has bolted. After all, some of them at fifteen have had more sexual partners than I have!

The one good thing, though, about taking a sex lesson, is that most people (particularly at fifteen) are interested in the subject! Imagine my surprise, then, when I was introduced to one class at a local school and a girl in the front row immediately said in a loud voice, 'This is going to be boring. We all know what you are going to say anyway!'

A little taken aback, I said, 'Oh really? Please tell me.'

'You are going to say that it is wrong to have sex and we should wait until we are married.' There were murmurs of support from other members of the class. It was obvious that she was not alone in thinking this way.

'If I promise,' I said, 'not to say those things, and I am as honest as I can be about what I think, will you listen to me?'

She gave a cautious OK (which basically meant that I had five minutes to prove myself, otherwise they would all switch off) and the lesson got going.

The first ten minutes looked at our sex-mad society. I had video and music clips, adverts, magazines, etc. We had a laugh at some of the absurd bits and debunked a few of Hollywood's sex myths (which the more sexually experienced in the class were quite open in affirming!). I even managed to demonstrate perfectly why advertisers use sexual imagery when I held up a particular poster and two boys at the back stood up to get a better look! After ten minutes we were at saturation point and some of them were beginning to realise, perhaps for the first time, just how sex mad our contemporary world really is.

Then we moved on to the down side: 'Society fans the flames without thinking of the consequences.' We looked at how many videos have rape scenes to boost their sales, and we read in worksheets of paedophile and abuse rings and the realities of the porn industry, as well as an article of a girl who fulfilled her dreams and slept with her pop idol, with crushing results. We looked at the terrifying reality of sexually transmitted diseases and the nightmare of 4.5 million abortions in the last thirty years. Then to a by now hushed class I said, 'And some of us here know from bitter experience how sex is not all it's cracked up to be.'

I talked about some of the fears and motives that

drive us into sexual relationships and summed up at the halfway point by saying, 'You can see why I am not satisfied that what we all think about sex actually works.' The class were with me now.

The next part of the lesson looked at some alternative views, including contrasting what we labelled the Victorian and the Hippie views and tried to see what was good, but also what was weak, about each.

Only after all this did I sense the class were ready to hear what I really thought. I told them that sex was fantastic and that far from being dirty and wrong, when they felt that indescribable excitement of sexual attraction, it was actually a gift from God. I talked about how I believe that we are made in God's image, which means we long to be loved and to be intimate with someone special. I talked about how we have ignored the Maker's instructions, though, and are now reaping the consequences of that; how in today's world we look to sexual partners for what only God can provide. Then with five minutes left I talked honestly about my own struggles with sexuality before giving some practical pointers to people who chose not to sleep around.

'Sex is, I believe, the contemporary religion substitute par excellence. Sex has supplanted religion in the imagination as a favourite way to the beyond. Sex is so often associated with pleasure in the popular press that its links with reproduction are almost forgotten.'[11]

The next day I had a phone call from the teacher. The

class had asked her to invite me back the following week! That next lesson, they had an hour's worth of questions ready for me and I tried to answer them as best I could. As a result of that, three of the class asked to see me privately and ended up attending the local church. As for me, the whole episode began to clarify some of what I had been thinking. There are a number of lessons to be learned.

1. PEOPLE THINK THEY KNOW WHAT WE ARE WANTING TO SAY, WHEN THEY DON'T

Like the girl in the front row, many adults today have a 'been there, got the tee-shirt' attitude about Christianity. They remember, perhaps, assemblies at school, scout and guide parades or singing in the choir, supplemented with the odd church christening, wedding and funeral, and they think they have 'done' Christianity. It is all part of being a once-Christian country. People might be more open to spiritual things now, but there is a feeling of having moved on from established Christian religion.

The trouble with that is that the public face of Christian religion so often copies the effect but loses the heart of the gospel. Now we face an uphill task. We have a vital message to tell, but people think they have heard it already, when they have not.

Søren Kierkegaard told the famous story of a clown. Each day he would go to the village and entertain the crowd with his antics. On one occasion, though, he could see that a fire had started behind the crowd. He frantically tried to warn his audience, but they thought it was just part of his show and roared with laughter. As a result, the village burned down. They too thought they knew what the clown was trying to say.

Among young people, though, there is an important difference. The vast majority of teens today have not rejected Jesus – they simply do not know enough about him to have done that. Peter Brierley, in his book *Reaching and Keeping Teenagers*, has shown, however, that they do see going to church as a children's activity enforced by parents, which any self-respecting teenager should have grown out of by now. In this sense, they share with adults a 'we have moved on from there' attitude towards Christianity.

2. EVANGELISM HAS TO START FURTHER BACK

The problem is that we are faced with a generation who are in effect self-destructing while at the same time feeling perversely self-sufficient. If we are to communicate the gospel effectively to this kind of world, we are going to have to take evangelism one step further back. We must recognise that people today will not consider Jesus until they have first discovered that what they believe is neither true, nor does it work.

Today's evangelistic process has to begin with exposing the lies of the world in which we live; unmasking the gods of this age, with all their pretence, so that this generation will sense their need to ask the questions which Jesus will provide the answers for.[12]

3. EVANGELISM TODAY OFTEN BEGINS WITH ISSUES

Today's society is interested in movements, not institutions. In politics, for example, we have seen the development of single-issue politics in recent years. People don't believe in big, overarching truths any more, but they will back a cause they believe in. The church needs to be sensitive to this agenda and have a much more flexible view of evangelism. In today's world some of the best opportunities arise out of first proving that Christianity has something helpful and credible to say into the issues of the day. Elaine Storkey talking on Radio 4's *Thought for the Day* about BSE, and Steve Chalke on GMTV at the time of Dunblane are good national media examples of this. On the personal level, it is what Willow Creek calls the 'felt needs of people', i.e. handling stress, bringing up our children, balancing the budget, maximising our marriage. If we prove that Christianity has something to say to these contemporary issues, the doorway is open to people's attention. One thing is for sure: if the church is going to respond to young people in today's world, it has to be seen to be responding to sexuality in our culture.

Thom Hopler suggests that history goes in waves and these waves are realities, though they are difficult to pin down in actual years. In the early years of each new wave the missionaries have to be different, e.g. Christian women taken captive by vikings, William Carey going it alone to India, etc. The early part of any of these waves sees new creative ways of getting the gospel out. We can be paralysed by fear, or we can seek out creative new means of dealing with these movements.

> I don't know what they will look like, but I believe that they are to be found by courageous Christians willing to try. We can and must take advantage of these forces that threaten to destroy us and use them to expand and strengthen God's Church.[13]

Summary of Chapter 9

The church does not have a problem with young people. The church has a problem with the gospel.

If the church takes the gospel seriously, it will inevitably take young people seriously as they are the single largest group of non-Christians regularly attending church.

When we do take young people seriously the church is helped in overcoming a number of barriers to evangelism in our world today.

- We are forced to recognise our own cultural blindness.
- We learn to preach a gospel more relevant to an issue-dominated society that has lost its grip on truth.
- Most of all we are reminded of the need to live that truth as well as preach it. Like it or not, in the post-modern world the church is the Christian apologetic.

10

Discipleship Essentials

The spirit of our age makes evangelism easier, but discipleship more difficult.[1]

In Chapter 2, we saw that Christian discipleship has been seriously undermined by our culture's values. In particular:

- rational faith;
- feeling faith;
- private faith;
- material faith.

This chapter looks at how the experiences of youth workers trying to disciple young people can help the wider church with some of these issues.

Incarnational-style discipleship

Very quickly after getting involved in youth ministry, I began to see that the only way to deal with peer pressure was to fight fire with fire.

I had noticed that residential work with young people – be it over a weekend house party or a summer camp – accomplished more in a matter of hours than three months of the normal youth programme. There was something of real lasting worth and value from these ventures that went far beyond the 'high' of simply being away together. They proved to be fast tracks in Christian growth and maturity.

As I reflected on this, I began to see that adolescent relationships are so all-encompassing and self-defining that for a young person to have any real chance of being discipled, the youth group had to be so good that it became the dominant peer group, the teenager's main anchor and reference point outside of the family. In practice, that is what happened on our residential trips, and it was this sense of community that we tried to replicate on a day-by-day, week-by-week basis. This had obvious dangers of cliquishness which we tried to guard against, but that understanding of the youth group as the alternative peer group was the model which we tried to develop.

As I was looking for a biblical model for what we ought to do, it became apparent that Christianity is better caught than taught. The discipling models that we are given in Scripture appear to suggest that Christian growth and maturity are the results of long-term relational investments. Moses and Joshua, Elijah and Elisha, Eli and Samuel, Paul and Timothy and, of course, Jesus and the disciples all have these traits. So much so that the Gospel of Mark sums up the disciples' initial calling as simply 'to be with him' (Mk 3:14). Truth, it seems, is more powerful modelled across a dining table than taught across a classroom.

Of course, this whole principle is encapsulated in the incarnation. God became Man and crossed the cosmic cultural barrier, not just to tell us the truth, but to *be* the truth. Jesus met people where they were in a way they understood – a walking, living example of a life that brings God pleasure.

The apostle Paul took this incarnational principle of Christianity very seriously in his church planting. Though he wrote many detailed letters teaching theology and correcting misunderstandings, he earthed all this teaching in the roots of relationship, even to churches that he had not as yet met! But to those he had met, he took the incarnational principle even further: 'We loved you so much that we were delighted to share with you not only the gospel of God but our lives as well, because you had become so dear to us' (1 Thess 2:8); 'Whatever you have learned or received or heard from me, or seen in me – put it into practice. And the God of peace will be with you' (Phil 4:9); 'Follow my example, as I follow the example of Christ' (1 Cor 11:1).

What incredible statements! Paul was not, however, some ego maniac. He was very well aware of his own failings (Rom 7:14–20) and compared with Christ he was but a poor reflection of God's purposes. Neither does Paul ever go as far as to say that he *became* Jesus to people. That goes beyond the teaching of the New Testament. Paul talks of *following* Christ, never *being* Christ. We cannot be Jesus to people (for Jesus is at the right hand of the Father). We can only be an example of what following Christ means. Nevertheless Paul understood the significance of incarnation; he understood the significance of learning by example. Ultimately he knew that truth comes in lives, not on paper.

It seems that the temptation throughout church history has been to attempt to short cut this process, to break down the sanctification into component parts and try to substitute a lack of relationship with books, conferences and sermons. By and large, it has not worked. As C. S. Lewis put it, 'The longest way round is (still) the shortest way home'!

Such a view turned my ideas about youth work upside down. A youth worker became someone who entered into the world of a teenager and made Jesus real by the way they lived. Our official role or activity in the youth programme was no more than a starting point for the real work. Programmes and events were only justified if they created an environment where quality relationships could be established. Supremely it meant that it was not so much what we said but who we were that communicated Christ.

If this model of youth work was to happen, the only way was to lead by example. From then on, youth ministry ceased to be a job and became my life. My primary task was to share my life with young people. Later my wife and I were to buy a bigger house with another member of the youth leadership team, simply so that we could operate in this lifestyle pattern more effectively and be more available and geographically closer to the teenagers with whom we were working.

Incarnational-style discipleship and the wider church

In today's church experience, there is much of value that we can learn from youth workers as they explore an incarnational style of ministry.

FELLOWSHIP

We have already seen in previous chapters how many feel isolated and lost in today's world and are looking for a sense of 'connectedness'. Sadly, when they encounter the church they so often find it a mirror image of the very thing they want to get away from – the impersonal institution. In a high-tech society, people are looking for a high-touch church which provides a sense of belonging in a world in which they feel lost. In simple terms, friendship is the vehicle of God's love.

The heavy bit

'The search for community is a quest for values to heal a fragmented humanity. In leadership, hierarchies are being flattened, the corporation style church which we are cloning cannot birth this transformational vision because they have no investment in context or place. We are looking for community. It is a new wineskin. The bottom line is that people want to belong, they want to deal with this unconnectedness.'[2]

Take the way many churches still have home groups, for example. When we are organised into groups and told to have fellowship, do we really expect this to produce the connectedness that people feel they need today? Isn't it more the biblical model that fellowship is more a byproduct of working together than a product of focused efforts? Paul's list of personal greetings in Romans 16 is a classic example of this – lasting friendships forged in the heat of mission.

Providing genuine fellowship for people is one of the biggest areas of tension for a modern church in a post-modern world. Perhaps it is more appropriate to see fellowship as a consequence of mission activity

THE BOTTOM LINE IS THAT PEOPLE WANT TO BELONG...

together, rather than something which should be targeted and sought after in its own right.

ACCOUNTABLE LEADERSHIP

One of the challenging aspects of incarnational-style ministry is the extent to which leaders have to be open and real. Because I wanted to develop a sense of mutual accountability and openness, I invited the group of teenagers to ask me how I was doing with God, as well as me asking them. There were times when they needed reminding and times when it was difficult to know quite what to say, but by and large it was a very helpful experience for the young people concerned. It seemed to lead to a healthy atmosphere of openness and accountability among the group, where people genuinely started taking responsibility for each other. Obviously there are weaknesses it would be inappropriate to share, but I have come to see that this mutual openness and accountability is a vital part of the discipling process. How else did the disciples know the anguished content of the Gethsemane prayer unless at a later date Jesus had chosen to tell them? No doubt, years later when they faced horrible deaths, it was a real encouragement to them that the Lord himself had been fearful too and that to be frightened was not a lack of faith or sinful. In this way, Jesus gives us an example of sharing appropriate needs for the strengthening of others.

So often I have listened to the tortured confessions of guilt from teenagers and begun my response very deliberately with, 'Yes, I struggle with that too.' Many times I have seen that simple phrase bring relief to someone's face, take weight off their shoulders and begin a process of forgiveness and healing for their soul.

'It's not that we aren't where we should be, it's that we are not what we should be where we are.'[3]

Incarnation in the culture

I found that because of this understanding that we were entering into their world, and not they into ours, an incarnational-style view of youth ministry brought with it an exciting prospect of trying to disciple people in their own culture.

This was comparatively easy for the kids of

Christian families. For them, youth culture was really only a veneer – genuine enough, but in reality only skin deep. They shared in the looks, but by and large not the values, of the world of their peers. They were still teenagers, of course, and therefore wanted to be perceived as different, but deep down their roots were largely the same as mine. In most cases, their parents had seen to it that society's influence had not gone too far beyond fashion styles, music and vegetarianism! A truly biblical, contextualised discipleship programme for these teenagers meant little more than quoting from chart songs, using video clips, keeping talks short and fast moving, and playing lots of games!

It was among the young people from non-Christian homes or even homes hostile to the Christian faith that the challenge of discipling within their culture was enormous. Even for the ones whose parents were sceptical and viewed this period of their lives as 'just a phase they are going through' it was tricky enough. Putting myself in their shoes was very hard. I constantly had to start further back if the gospel was to make sense. But to communicate with those who had been abused, were using drugs, were promiscuous, were illiterate, came from bad homes or were involved in crime was very hard indeed. It was something, I confess, I never really came to terms with.

James, the friend I spoke of in Chapter 3, was again my doorway to understanding here. For someone dressed as he was, with his very limited reading and writing ability, church was even more intimidating and alien to him than school. On the occasions when he did come, he just hated it. I soon realised that going to church was positively unhelpful in introducing James to Jesus.

So we set up a small group at our flat for him and his friends, and I tried to spend time with him and his family. James and I played sport together and he learned to swim. I used to try and help him on his paper round when I could and he helped me out on more than one occasion with housework or shopping. He was chosen to play rugby for his school once, and it was the most important appointment of the year for me. It was just about the only success of his entire school career and I would not have missed it for the world.

In those early days of our relationship I felt that I had to challenge much of his lifestyle and behaviour, because it was so chaotic and destructive. Pretty soon I found that all that did was put up barriers between us. After a while issues like smoking, language, diet, lifestyle, homework and budgeting all became issues which, while I consciously tried to model an alternative, I chose not to speak about with him as they would only get in the way of what really mattered. I was learning that Jesus works from the inside out, not the outside in.

The greatest practical problem, and the biggest obstacle in our relationship, was our understanding of time. I was part of a large church, with many responsibilities including other staff, and everything revolved around my diary. James didn't have a diary. He didn't 'book in' anything. He lived his life on the spur of the moment.

Ever wary of dependency, I made sure that while our relationship remained strong, we did things together with other teenagers, as well as involving and introducing him to other friends in the church (something which incidentally he greatly appreciated, commenting on more than one occasion that he had made more friends since he had met me!).

Over the years we went through a great deal together. There were the different stages of adolescence, of course (including a period when he would not come round for a meal until it was dark, in case people thought he was babyish!). He came on holiday with us and on one occasion we took him to Spring Harvest, where he spent the whole week staring at the sea (he had never seen it before). On his fourteenth birthday we threw a surprise party with all his mates. When we brought out the cake and candles, his eyes filled with tears – something I had never seen before. He explained afterwards that he had never had a birthday cake.

During this time, faith was naturally part of our relationship. I am sure he eventually understood the gospel, despite my inability to tell the simple story (looking back I always used to complicate it). We certainly saw our prayers answered – mainly when he was in trouble. At times he was bitter about his life and refused to help himself, but most of the time he was a cheerful, fun-loving lad, who just wanted to belong somewhere.

It was in his last year of school that things went badly wrong. One day, a lad followed him around all day, insulting him for the clothes he wore. The last lesson of the day was woodwork, and once again the taunts came. This time James snapped, and he picked up a piece of wood and hit the boy. As a result he was permanently excluded from school.

I tried very hard to get him back into school. I tried to get him home tuition. I tried to find him an apprenticeship, but there was nothing available. Home all day when his friends were at school, he began to get involved with a group of travellers. Here, in a very different way, James found a sense of belonging, and in less than a year he left home for life on the road.

Now when we occasionally meet it is at the pub (though not one of his regular haunts, because, as he explained to me once, 'If we had bother, a "soft life" like you would be no good to me!'). His life is full of trouble, prejudice and restlessness, yet this only seems to deepen the camaraderie with his fellow travellers. We both reminisce over what we went through together and he assures me: 'I still remember what you taught me.' But he simply leaves it at that. At the end of the evening he goes back to his world and I go back to mine.

Through the heartbreak of it all, however, some things began to become clear to me. So much of what happened at the church over the ten years that I was there was exciting and good. We saw many youngsters come to faith and go on to be disciples. Several of those who were not from Christian homes are still walking with God and some are in full-time service around the world. But there were a number of young people, of whom James was one, who simply did not fit into the church youth group model. They were so different that they needed an entirely different approach.

Looking back, we failed to disciple them in their culture. If I had the chance again, I think I would have released some of my best youth workers from all church responsibilities and encouraged them to work in a detached way on the street with young people like James.[4]

At the end of the day, what James was longing for was love and acceptance – somewhere he could feel at home and be secure. While he enjoyed good levels of friendship with myself and a few others, he never felt part of the church community. An organised, structured church could never provide that for a young person like James. I mourn the loss of James to the church, but the whole experience made me realise that to truly disciple people in their culture requires flexible models for doing and being God's church.

It is at this crucial point of incarnational leadership that youth work is at its most prophetic to the wider church. When our attempts at Christian discipleship are so often undermined by our culture's hidden values, incarnational leadership can bring real understanding and a realigning to biblical truth, by challenging our assumptions about church.

Rational and feeling faith

There is, of course, no complete answer to the rationalising and emotionalising of faith. To suggest otherwise would be foolishness. However, working with young people does undoubtedly help point towards at least some of the answers.

First, because we are working from the perspective of affirming what is good and challenging what is wrong in youth culture, it means that young people in our churches should be growing up from the start very much more aware than previous generations of the cultural specs they are wearing. This has to be the biggest and most fundamental issue. The reason why the rationalising and emotionalising of faith has been such a powerful influence is that most Christians are not aware that they even have a set of cultural specs in the first place and are even less conscious that this colours their understanding and experience of faith. A constructive view of culture leads to people being more aware of the culture of which they are part.

Secondly, because the youth work model is incarnational in its approach, it is by definition very people centred. In today's post-modern society, where elements of both rationalism and emotionalism are commonly found, much has to do with the individual's temperament and disposition. Some are by nature more objective, others more emotional. In a people-centred approach to discipleship, there is more chance of personality bias one way or the other being picked up and addressed. It also takes seriously the idea that Christianity is better caught than taught and has the chance to be modelled more appropriately by the youth leaders themselves.

Private faith

Once we understood that Christian youth leadership meant entering into the world of a teenager and making Jesus real, we set about our research. We soon discovered that a teenager's world revolved around school and family. From this time on, these were our entry points into explaining what it meant to be a Christian. What do you do when Mum and Dad are arguing? How do you cope when your little brother annoys you? What do you do when you are bullied; when you can't do your homework; when you don't get into the school team? These issues became the essential entry points for learning to think in a Christian way, applying biblical principles to everyday situations.

We were discovering by accident that incarnational

leadership naturally leads to culturally relevant discipleship and that in turn culturally relevant discipleship naturally leads to a more public and robust view of faith. What do I do when my friend is being bullied? What do I say to my friends when they are trying pot? What do I do when my friends are having casual sex? Take the principle of discipling in someone's natural culture seriously and faith will struggle to remain private. Perhaps one of the reasons why faith has in so many cases become privately engaging but publicly irrelevant, is that our induction in it has not been biblically incarnational, so faith is removed from the real world.

Putting it succinctly, incarnation leads to contextualisation, which leads to relevance in the public world.

Exposing dualism

It was on this journey to publicly relevant faith that questions were raised by some older Christians about a programme which included subjects like 'Bringing up your parents', 'Ultimate sex' and 'Does saint mean swot?'. It was through subsequent conversations that I first came to understand a major theological problem facing the church today, which previously I had only read about. For lurking behind their unease that these subjects were too worldly was a very shadowy customer indeed – dualism. Ultimately it was understanding dualism which explained to me why Evangelicals have had such a difficult time with the issue of culture.

CAREFUL DUALISM

Dualism itself should not be a dirty word. It basically means 'when two subjects cannot be reduced into one'. So there are areas of the Christian faith where careful dualism needs to be affirmed. Take God and creation, for example. We do not believe that a mountain or a river is God to be worshipped. God made the world, but is distinct from it. Anything less and our worship becomes confused. Paul upholds another important dualism in Romans 6–8 when he contrasts the work of the sinful nature and the Spirit.

CARELESS DUALISM

The trouble comes when careful dualism becomes careless dualism; when biblical dualism becomes cultural dualism; when a simplistic mindset of two worlds, the physical and the spiritual, becomes the filter through which we read the Bible and see all of life itself. Everything then has to be either ruled in or out, of God or of the world, sacred or secular. Such a black-and-white universe does not exist and owes more to Plato than it does to Christ, but its enduring attraction is that it makes life so much simpler!

Simple it might be, but harmless it is not! Thriving on half-truths and a basic human desire to have everything neatly labelled, careless dualism left un-challenged can completely undermine Christianity's role in the world, because it whispers to us all the time that we should not really be there.

DUALISM'S DOUBLE WHAMMY

Dualism's sinister power lies in the fact that it is so much a part of both our non-Christian worldview and our traditional church thinking that its specs are never noticed. Our non-Christian specs are powerful enough, but when these are combined with the misguided thought of the church, dualism becomes the double whammy that catches out most of us at one time or another. Let us look at this double whammy in more detail.

Dualism in the Western world today

Since the Enlightenment, there has been a false divide in the Western world between faith and reason which has dominated the way we all think.

The Enlightenment ('for all its real light', as Newbigin so wonderfully puts it) over-emphasised human reason so much that in the end anything which could not be objectively examined was not accepted as true. Faith was held to be outside this realm of testing, so a false dualism took hold. Faith was not the same as truth any more.

This climate of 'unreasonable reason' pressured many churches to take sides, either emphasising thinking at the expense of experience, or emphasising experience at the expense of common sense! Meanwhile, for the vast majority of people in the Western world, the perception was simply that the men in white coats and the men in dog collars had had a scrap, and the men in white coats had won! Science was now fact and religion speculation.

Dualism in the church today

If dualism in the world was not enough to cause us problems, at the same time dualism has strong roots in the church. It was particularly after the conversion of Emperor Constantine that dualism became a problem. Suddenly at peace with the state after years of persecution, the church quickly found itself caught up in supporting the government instead of holding to its prophetic and evangelistic calling.

Many committed Christians, frustrated by this 'worldly compromise', came out to start alternative churches and in doing so over-emphasised the 'come out and be separate' nature of true faith. From then on, it would appear that the more devout the movement, the more dualistic its disciples! They had a clear upstairs/downstairs worldview, where things were either of the flesh or of the Spirit, and there was an emphasis on abstaining from worldly pleasures and pursuing a higher, less compromised spiritual life. Ironically, far from being 'in the world but not of it', they became 'of the world and not in it', all because of dualism! In many ways today we still live with this legacy of thought.

A case of careless dualism…

'I cannot believe that a person who has ever known the love of God can relish a secular novel. Let me visit your chamber, your parlour, or wherever you keep your books. What is here? Byron, Scott, Shakespeare and a host of triflers and blasphemers of God.'[5]

A biblical response to dualism

All this is somewhat ironic, given that the Bible writers went out of their way to challenge careless dualism.

John's Gospel, for example, was written to explain the Christian message to Greeks seeped in a dualistic philosophy. With that audience, he deliberately chose to use the word *logos* to describe Jesus. The *logos* was part of the sacred world to the Greeks, so the opening words of the book struck a genuine chord of familiarity with them: 'In the beginning was the Word, and the Word was with God, and the Word was God. He was with God in the beginning' (Jn 1:1–2).

No sooner had common ground been established, however, than John started pushing the boundaries of his readers' understanding: 'He was in the world' (v.10), and then sending shock waves through the system with: 'The Word became flesh' (v.14). Four carefully chosen words which for all time stamped Christianity's refusal to fit into a dualistic under-standing of the universe.

The apostle Paul, likewise, set about challenging this underlying two-world assumption of many of his readership:

See to it that no-one takes you captive through hollow and deceptive philosophy, which depends on human tradition and the basic principles of this world rather than on Christ (Col 2:8).

Since you died with Christ to the basic principles of this world, why, as though you still belonged to it, do you submit to its rules: 'Do not handle! Do not taste! Do not touch!'? These are all destined to perish with use, because they are based on human commands and teachings. Such regulations indeed have an appearance of wisdom, with their self-imposed worship, their false humility and their harsh treatment of the body, but they lack any value in restraining sensual indulgence... Whatever you do, work at it with all your heart, as working for the Lord, not for men, since you know that you will receive an inheritance from the Lord as a reward. It is the Lord Christ you are serving (Col 2:20–23; 3:23–24).

Paul seems to treat dualism not as if it was a question of either/or, but of both/and! Everything in creation was made good (1 Tim 4:4), but it has also been marred by sin and so is fallen and bad (2 Cor 6:14–18; 7:1; Rom 3:23). However, through Christ, God has acted to rescue the world and reconcile it to himself (2 Cor 5:19). Jesus himself referred to this tension of a fallen and yet created humanity in his phrase 'You, though you are evil, know how to give good gifts to your children' (Mt 7:11). For the Christian, then, careless dualism is not an option; rather the Bible calls us to live holding in tension this fallen and yet God-created world order.

C. S. Lewis sums up the Bible's refusal to slip into dualism and yet not dismiss it out of hand quite wonderfully: 'There is no neutral ground in the universe. Every square inch, every split second, is claimed by God and counter claimed by Satan.'[6]

Dualism through church history

Fortunately there have been a number of thinking Christians through the centuries, alert to the dangers of casual dualism. In his excellent book on fashion, Mike Starkey notes how Calvin, despite the fact that many of his followers were to become world denyers, offered a positive framework for understanding the material world, describing it even as a 'theatre of glory'.

For the Puritans there was not the war between the spiritual and material that their reputation for piety suggests. They had 'a hearty earthiness, based on the understanding that in the routine, practical tasks of daily life, were the arenas where we meet God'.[7]

Others, too, have eloquently and powerfully spoken against casual dualism.

> When St Paul says 'Come out and be separate', he did not mean that Christians ought to take no interest in anything on earth except religion. To neglect science, art, literature and politics – to read nothing which is not directly spiritual – to know nothing about what is going on among mankind and never to look at a newspaper – to care nothing about the government of one's own country and to be utterly indifferent to the persons who guide its councils and make its laws – all this may seem very right and proper in the eyes of some people. But I take leave to think that it is an idle, selfish neglect of duty.[8]

> 'When the church ceases to be concerned with the world then it ceases to hear God speak to it. For God's conversation with the church is a conversation about the world and the church must be willing to converse about the world if it is to converse with God. It is the world which is the direct object of God's action. He made it, He loved it, He saved it, He will judge it through Jesus Christ. Indeed, a church that is disobedient to its commission to go to the world becomes a menace to the world itself.'[9]

Dualism today

The trouble is that the biblical worldview is far more difficult to hold to than a careless dualistic one.

Dualism is neatly labelled, whereas a more biblical worldview requires us to live with paradox and tension.

Chris Seaton, in his helpful book *Your Mind Matters*, highlights six areas (all beginning with *E*!) where careless dualism still holds sway in Christian thinking today.

ETHICS

Careless dualism leads to an unbalanced Christian ethic, where we are strong on private morality, but weak on public truth. As a consequence, we are far more comfortable talking about personal issues like abortion and pornography than public ones like education and employment.

EVANGELISM

When the only thing that we can say about the world is that it is utterly fallen, going into it (Mt 28) becomes more a question of ingrab rather than outreach – rescuing individuals into the church rather than seeing the church changing society.

ECOLOGY

If the world is only fallen, then it is doomed to destruction anyway, and the environment is not a priority for Christians. After all, we are about saving souls, not whales!

ESCHATOLOGY

An over-emphasis on a fallen world can easily lead to a preoccupation with future things like the Second Coming of Christ and revival. If we are not very careful, this becomes a serious cop-out, a head-in-the-sand mentality of 'Jesus is going to come back one day and will make everything right, so just sit tight' rather than the biblical 'thy kingdom come, thy will be done *on earth*, as it is in heaven'. To pray for revival and/or for Christ to come again, without doing anything about it, is actually a form of escapism.

EMPLOYMENT

Our upstairs/downstairs legacy of life leads to honouring so-called full-time Christian workers at the expense of recognising that all Christians are full time by definition of being Christian.

ENGAGEMENT

Rather than seeing the arts as humanity's inherited creativeness from God, when we see the world as only fallen, the arts are relegated to frivolous entertainment to be avoided by Christians. The cinema is not called the 'sin-ema' for nothing!

Ultimately, careless dualism paralyses Christians into a state of spiritual schizophrenia, seeking a label for everything, rather than living with tension in a world caught between the now and the not yet. Howard Snyder sees dualism's influence in the church today primarily affecting our focus of attention. If we succumb to careless dualism, we focus on the church in the world, whereas those living with a more biblical worldview tend to focus on the kingdom of God instead. He put it like this: 'Church people think about how to get people into the church, kingdom people think about how to get the church into the kingdom. Church people worry that the world might change the church, kingdom people work to see the church change the world.'[10]

This was exactly the issue we faced in the youth programme. Incarnational-style discipleship had led to a robust, publicly relevant faith which focused young Christians on changing their world. Older Christians, without that incarnational understanding, had a more 'private' faith and, as a result, were much more concerned about the danger of the world polluting the church.

Material faith

When every aspect of life is understood to be God's, Western materialism inevitably comes under his spotlight.

Following a youth weekend away, which had highlighted the appalling needs of the two thirds world and compared it with the wealth and affluence of the West, the youth group really took up the challenge of becoming world Christians. Thanks to the input of a team from the Salvation Army led by Phil Wall, they coined the phrase the MAD Team (MAD standing for Make A Difference).

They started with themselves. I watched them form small accountability groups where they would confess their sins to each other and ask each other to take responsibility in prayer and advice for the way they handled their sexuality and their money. I watched them start sharing clothes and resources so that they could give the money they would have otherwise spent to third world related issues. It was fantastic to see!

During this period came one of the most enjoyable

moments of my ten years of youth ministry. A group of young people came round for coffee one evening. They had just spent the last three hours 'blitzing a house' (cleaning it from top to bottom) so that it was fit for an old man to return home to after a period in hospital. This was something that Jez, a sixteen-year-old lad in the group, had arranged completely on his own. There was not an adult in sight and none of the youth team had even known that it was taking place. The group had, by themselves, decided that this was something Christians ought to be doing and had simply got on with the job. By all accounts (and as you would expect they were pretty graphic!) the house had been in a terrible state with human and animal faeces in several rooms and they had to buy treble the quantity of disinfectant that they had anticipated! Nevertheless, they eventually got the place clean so that the man could return from hospital. Jez was the hero that night. Not only had he organised the whole thing, but he had led by example and volunteered to do the toilet himself! As I heard them laughing and talking that evening and sensing among them a feeling of accomplishment, I was very proud to be part of what God was doing in that group.

Then came the awkward bit. They started asking questions about what they could actually do in terms of direct action to improve the lot of people in the two thirds world. As I tried to explain that it wasn't as simple as it first appeared, I was met with a barrage of 'why nots'! I was forced to admit that my culturally conditioned cynicism was further from the biblical text than their simple idealism and as we worked through the issues together, idealism and realism met in an understanding that we could not solve everything, but we could do something. We could make a difference. So the Ethiopian MAD Project was born.

Over the next few years it was to result in twice taking groups of young people out to the slums of Addis Ababa, to experience first hand the squalor and degradation of some of the worst slum areas in Africa. While we did some work out there and tried to encourage people as best we could, the main purpose of our visits was to make a video to use for fundraising once we returned.

As the young people prepared to go out, worked hard to raise their air fares, spoke of the traumas of the visit upon their return and were brave enough to lead whole school assemblies, as well as teach lessons about their experiences, many adults in the church shared with me how challenged they were personally by the courage and boldness of the young people concerned. Some were challenged to give sacrificially. Two adults even gave up their normal jobs to live out more directly the priorities we were all learning about. Over time, the whole of the church was galvanised into action for the sake of the marginalised in our world. The MAD Project soon ceased to be simply a youth project and encompassed the whole of the church family. To date the church has raised in excess of £25,000 towards the work of the Christians in the slums.

When many of our churches today are held back in witness of the gospel simply because of the grip materialism has on our lives – when our understanding of the nature of God's love is compromised by our insistence of dividing evangelism and social action as if we can cut and paste with God's character – perhaps it is time to sit at the feet of those who maybe don't see the multi-nationals and the trade deficits as the giants we do, but armed with little more than some biblical principles and youthful idealism, go off to fight for justice.

After ten years of working with young people, I am convinced that we dismiss their youthful idealism at our peril. We have much to listen to and learn from.

The heavy bit

'Having has replaced being... Want becomes need. Consumption is the source of meaning. To hide it we have adopted a language of convenience again. We don't talk about debt and the damage we are doing to future generations. What do we call it? We call it credit. Credit cards are a status symbol. We treat debt as credit as if it is good.'[11]

HAVING HAS REPLACED BEING...

Summary of Chapter 10

Working with young people in their peer groups forces us to take the incarnational style of biblical discipleship seriously. That means that we learn to enter their world, not insist that they enter ours.

This not only helps Christians grow up more aware of culture's influence on their lives, but also encourages a more public and robust attitude to their faith, which in turn exposes careless dualistic thinking so prevalent in the church.

In short, incarnational-style discipleship is the single biggest factor in helping the church out of its culture trap.

I I

Educational Essentials

He who learns from one occupied in learning drinks from a running stream. He who learns from one who has learned all he has to teach, drinks the green mantle of the standing pool.[1]

You can't work with young people for very long without recognising that school is second only to family in its life-shaping influence upon young people. For any church giving priority to work with teenagers, school therefore has to become an important area of their involvement. And once this happens, there are things for the church to learn.

School – a doorway to the wider community

Schools are products of their communities. All the strengths and weaknesses of a particular area are reflected in a school. If an area is economically depressed, for example, then that lack of finance is inevitably going to be seen in the standard of school uniforms, the availability of money for sports equipment and the level of financial support that the PTA can provide. If an area is multi-cultural, so will the school be, and if an area is violent then the school will not be immune from that problem either. In short, schools are micro-communities, mirror images of the areas from which they draw their pupils.

This means that schools can provide a number of benefits to any church taking its input into school life seriously. The first and most obvious: get to know your school and you get to know your community. In fact schools can be a tremendous help in first getting to grips with an area. As I became more involved with my local school, I realised that it acted as a magnet, an access point for many statutory and business organisations. My first contact with adult education, sports clubs, counsellors, local businesses and police, for example, all came through meetings at school.

If we take on board this idea that school is a mirror image of the wider community, its make-up and attitudes, the church has a lot more to learn as it reflects on the nature of its relationship with school.

Plausibility versus credibility

I well remember my first approach to the local school to see if I could take an assembly. I had only been a youth minister for three months and I was keen to stress my commitment to the educational process and to distance myself from any view that saw church in school as a means of proselytising. Unknown to me, though, a few years previously the school had been hit by an irresponsible evangelist who had been very insensitive in a school assembly, with fairly dire consequences. As a result, years later, the head teacher was extremely guarded and non-committal with me. It eventually took a reference from another school before I had the chance to do even an assembly!

Having survived this first hurdle, however, I was invited again, and within a year or two I was a regular visitor to the school, teaching lessons, taking assemblies and involved in the school pastoral care system, as well as lunchtime clubs. One development followed another as the level of trust and relationship deepened. Slowly, what was happening was that the perception of the church held by the senior staff was being changed. We were now being seen as fellow community providers. In effect, our schools work was winning back lost ground in post-Christian Britain.

Looking back now, this level of trust and involvement that the church established with the local school was crucial to the success of a number of projects. Our schools work established a level of community credibility and trust which could not have been achieved any other way. Parents tended to take their lead from the school. If the school was prepared to trust us with their pupils, then so would the parents.

Once again, the youth worker's experience in school has a lot to teach the wider church about the miscommunication that happens between God's people and society. When I first met the school head teacher I was only concerned about the credibility of the Christian message in the educational setting. However, his interest in me was not about the credibility of what I would say, but the plausibility of who I was. Churches so often approach evangelism as if the credibility of our beliefs is all that counts, but as with my first contact with the school, it is not the credibility of the message, but rather the plausibility of who we are that is the main issue. This can only be overcome by building relationships over time.

Evangelism and education

I had always been taught that to evangelise directly was an abuse of the educational context. It was the job of schools to educate, the job of churches to evangelise. However, as I taught a multi-faith syllabus and as I taught life's ultimate issues, I discovered that good education is evangelistic. As I encouraged pupils to think deeply about their lives and evaluate the different belief systems for themselves, and to think about life's ultimate questions, the process was by definition evangelistic in that it naturally led people to search for truth and so took them steps closer to Christ. It totally legitimately allowed the claims of Christ to be critically examined and weighed up against other religious views.

Here lies another exciting insight into our evangelistic work in our current cultural setting. If good education is evangelistic, the church ought to be thinking about running adult education classes at local colleges and schools, helping people to think through life's ultimate issues. Or how about parenting courses for our communities – practically orientated, but with enough about love, forgiveness and identity to set people thinking about the bigger issues? Here, perhaps, are some of the pioneer paths for evangelism at the turn of the millennium.

CU or lessons?

One of the more revealing insights from my involvement with school, though, came as the constraints on my time forced me to choose my priorities. I could either give priority to supporting the small number of Christians who met at lunchtime in the school Christian Union, or I could, through continuing my lesson input, work with a larger number of young people not in any way connected with the church. On the basis that the Christian teenagers had churches to support them, and without fully appreciating the significance of the decision I was making, I chose the latter.

It was very interesting how this move was perceived among some of my Christian friends in the church. Supporting church kids at the school's Christian Union was viewed as a legitimate Christian ministry. Teaching RE clearly was not! Once again I was encountering the careless dualism that hides behind so much Christian thought.

School is where it counts

I am often asked what has been the highlight of my years in youth ministry. Without doubt, one of the best moments was at the end of one summer term, when I received a call from a form teacher whom I barely knew. 'I want to thank you for my best year in teaching so far,' she said. I was bewildered because I had never even taught her group. 'My form class this year has had five young people who have started attending your church. I have watched their lives change and in turn witnessed the atmosphere of the whole tutor group change. It has been a most wonderful year.'

There have been many great moments over ten years of youth ministry, with memorable weekends away, times when God's presence was tangible in meetings, the joy of seeing young people converted and great projects come to fulfilment. However, that phone call still stands out as one of the best moments of all. Ultimately, Christian ministry has to be measured by the salt-and-light effect that Christians have in their world: 'By their fruits you shall know them.'

Learning to teach

It is not only in our interaction with school life that the church has things to learn. We have so much to benefit from in thinking through the educational process itself.

One of the greatest challenges facing all youth workers is how to teach God's word to young people. Just how do you encourage 'the word of God to dwell in you richly' (Col 3:16) in a mixed age and mixed ability group, who are in the main not that keen on more education?

Neither do we have the opportunity to teach them for very long. We normally do not have more than four years before young people move away to further education or out to work. In reality, it is a very small window of opportunity.

'It is a good thing that separation must come, otherwise that inner strength that is the purpose of education will not be strengthened.'[2]

Faced with these challenges as a youth worker, I sought to clarify in my mind the priorities for balanced biblical teaching. I was soon to realise that thinking about good education brings principles that are as valuable in the house group and the pulpit as they are in the youth group.

GOOD OLD TIM

As we turned the corner she was lying on the path in obvious agony. It was late evening and we were returning from a long walk on yet another church youth weekend away. The youth group rushed to the lady's assistance. She explained that while out jogging she had twisted her ankle and was now incapable of putting any weight on it at all. A cursory glance showed that her ankle was very swollen, and she would not let anybody touch it.

Little did they know it, but the young people were now unwittingly engaged in one of our more creative and valuable 'teaching times'! The lady was acting, the swelling was nothing more than cotton wool and the next five minutes were about to enter group folklore!

While the teenagers were discussing what to do, I said to the lady: 'I'm terribly sorry, but we've paid good money to come on this weekend and if we help you now we will miss our tea. What we'll do is hurry back to the centre and let them know where you are.' (All the youth leaders had been briefed to say nothing and simply follow me as I started to stride away!)

As you can imagine, the young people were somewhat bewildered and not a little indignant. After about twenty paces I turned and with as much authority as I could muster, said, 'Come on, you really must come. It's the best way to help.' To my horror a large group of the younger ones started to follow – grumbling but nevertheless doing what I said. This was not in my plan, but I was committed now! A few steps further on I turned and insisted that the others follow. At this point the majority of the group, embarrassed and angry (some even apologising to the lady on the ground), started to follow. I was just wondering what I was going to do next when Tim, one of the eldest boys, who had not left the lady's side, shouted in a very loud voice, 'Andy, this is wrong.'

Not a little relieved, I gathered the youth group around the lady and said, 'If you think I have just made a mistake, please stand on my right.' En masse they jumped at the chance to register their disapproval. Then I said, 'And if you were really prepared to do something about it, stay there.' They became very quiet and thoughtful as the penny dropped and they slowly all walked over to my left, leaving only Tim.

'We have spent the whole weekend learning about Christians making a difference in the world for God,' I said. 'If you can't do it here, what hope is there when we get home?' With that, I helped the lady up. It was only as she started to walk that the kids realised that it had all been a set up. I seem to remember I got rather muddy on the way home, but it was worth it. It was a lesson that none of us ever forgot!

CLARIFY THE PURPOSE

My first goal was to equip teenagers with how to think as Christians in a non-Christian world. This is very different from teaching them what they ought to think. True Christian education is teaching people how to think, not what to think. The Bible says that the truth shall set us free, so true Christian thinking should be characterised by openness and questioning, and a humble delight in truth revealed. 'Simplistic legalism never creates mature disciples; rather one of the vital tasks before the contemporary church is to train all of us, but especially our children, to critique and evaluate all around us.'[3]

The problem then arose of actually recognising when people truly knew and understood something they had been taught. Respected educationalist John Holt helps clarify this in his book *How Children Fail*. He argues that to really know something we must be able to:

- state it in our own words;
- give examples of it;
- recognise it in various circumstances;
- see the connection between it and other ideas and facts;
- make use of it in various ways;
- foresee some of its consequences;
- state its opposite or converse.

We know something, he concluded, when we understand why.[4]

CLARIFY THE PROCESS

When people acquire knowledge they progress through the following six stages:

UNAWARENESS   AWARENESS   INTEREST

ACCEPTANCE   CONVICTION   COMMITMENT

But we make a mistake if we focus exclusively on the style and content of what is being taught.

For example, social acceptance is critical to learning. This is because the single most important issue in learning is the ability to enquire. To enquire requires confidence, and confidence only comes through feeling accepted and comfortable within the group. The learning environment, then, is as important as the teaching content when it comes to education.

Children fail
● when they are afraid;
● when they are disappointing or displeasing adults;
● when they are bored;
● when it is trivial or dull;
● when they are confused;
● when words or ideas are above them;
● when the setting is unstable.

Another educational tool which may be helpful in youth work, as well as to the wider church, is the stepping method. This is a teaching aid designed to cope with a mixed ability group. It provides people with a structure of work (like a worksheet, for example) which gives maximum access to everyone by setting easy tasks to begin with and gradually getting harder, so that people are then free to study up to their appropriate level of ability. Another model is to teach a steady progression of ideas, but using a variety of stimuli to generate thought about the particular subject. Both of these education tools are fairly easily incorporated even into a standard sermon and even more easily into home-group material, etc.

Teaching organically

In his book *The Gospel Exploded*, Bob Mayo documents the ups and downs of trying to teach street teenagers in Bermondsey about Christ.

He was to discover that there was a massive difference in the way that young people on the street and teenagers in the church were best taught. 'I had been taught that discovering Jesus followed on from understanding Jesus. By contrast, what we began to teach the young people of the street was that understanding follows on from discovery.' Mayo realised that an organic approach was more helpful than an informational approach. In other words, 'Christians pray' is information; 'try talking to God yourself' is organic. 'Christians worship in church' is information; 'come and sing' is organic. By trying to teach prayer and worship, Mayo argues, we only complicate and confuse 'the most natural thing in the world'. Organic knowledge also has the advantage that it is self-feeding rather than being dependent on outside input.

On top of this organic education, Mayo discovered that simple story-telling was the best way forward for young people on the street to grasp the implications of the gospel. He constantly found himself having to resist the temptation to explain, and simply tell the Bible story. This way the Bible became more real and alive to teenagers because they were given the freedom to interpret the story for themselves. Mayo was in effect discovering on the streets of London a principle that many a missionary has discovered before him.

In order for this approach to work, however, it required an environment that was spontaneous and unstructured and that made itself up around what everyone wanted to know. Informal education required an informal setting.

Balanced teaching

I am indebted to Nick Pollard of the Solent Christian Trust and the Damaris Project for his incisive thinking about the nature of genuine Christian education.

DIDACTIC VERSUS CRITICAL

When debate rages in education about the didactic versus the critical method, Christians have to question whether either of them is an appropriate way of communicating Christian truth.

The traditional didactic method goes back to Plato, where a teacher teaches and the student listens and learns. The critical method, however, is rooted in the Enlightenment, where dogma was replaced by reason. This influenced education to the extent that teachers were now encouraging students to explore and find truth for themselves. The 1967 Plowden Report moved schools towards this latter view.

Both approaches are based on a different view of truth, and both views are inadequate from a Christian perspective. The didactic method tends towards a dogmatic view of truth: I know it and I will tell you about it. The critical method tends towards a relativist view of truth: no one has the monopoly on truth, so let us discover our own truth together. We must build a Christian model of truth, says Pollard, if we are to have truly Christian education.

Christian truth is obviously not relativist, but neither is it didactic. God has not revealed *all* truth to us and the truth he has revealed is in part hidden by our fallen human minds. There is absolute truth, but it is only God who holds it. So Christian education is God-centred and both teacher and pupil are trying to discover truth together. It starts with the teacher, but it is not dogmatic, and the student critiques and responds, all the while keeping the notion of truth as something to be discovered as we try to love God with our minds.

MODERN VERSUS POST-MODERN

Once again the Bible maintains an exquisite sense of balance when it comes to the modern/post-modern debate about words and pictures and their relationship to meaning.

> The visual dominates, the verbal recedes. Images replace words, words and images are pushed into opposition. It is crazy, though. God created them both. The original word and the ultimate image were in total harmony. God intended them to relate. Words inform us through our minds, images affect us through our eyes. Images call for recognition, words provide understanding. Jesus Christ was at once the Word and the Image of the Invisible God. He was the Word and He spoke God's truth and anyone who had seen Him, the Image, had seen the Father. The sight of a man dying was neither self-explanatory, nor left to create its own impression, it needed God's Word to reveal its meaning. Since Word and Image went together in Him, they cannot be opposed. Jesus did many miraculous signs, but without His interpretation their significance was lost.[5]

The perfect Teacher

There is nothing like being faced with a bunch of stroppy fourteen-year-olds who don't want to learn, to make the Christian youth worker ask the question, 'How would Jesus teach this group?'

As we learn about learning from the gospels, a number of things become apparent about Jesus' teaching style:

- Learning is centred on the learner, not the subject. Jesus communicated truth differently, depending on his audience (see for example Lk 10:25–37; Mk 10:17–25).
- Learning seemed to happen in a rhythm of action and reflection. For example, 54 per cent of his recorded encounters were initiated by questions.
- Learning had defined objectives (Mk 3:13–15).
- It took place in a community and the friction within that community added to the learning dynamic (Lk 22:24).
- Jesus' teaching often took place in an atmosphere of affirmation and expectancy (Mk 1:17; Jn 1:42).
- Jesus' style of teaching was not about the transmission of impersonal fact, but rather the transformation of a person (Mt 7:24).
- Learning was inseparably related to everyday life (e.g. Mt 10:29; 11:3; 12:10).
- Learning was aided by enforcement and repetition (Mk 8:29–33). The hardest lessons, it seems, need to be repeated.
- Jesus told stories. There are sixty-three parables in the gospels and only four of them are explained. Jesus trusted the inductive process, in sharp

contrast to the Pharisees who were orthodox and deductive. Jesus' stories were the point, their simplicity was their chief charm.

- Jesus asked questions to make people think and involved people practically, that lessons might be reinforced (Mt 4:19). These practical sessions were followed up with debriefs and retreats for more learning (e.g. Lk 9, a rhythm of action and reflection).

- Fundamentally, Jesus' style of education takes place through studying a living example (Jn 13).

- Jesus was an informal teacher. He used opportunities as they arose, especially questions, to take people deeper in their understanding of the kingdom.

In their book *Learning to Preach Like Jesus*, Ralph and Greg Lewis suggest that Jesus' teaching style took account of what we understand today are the functions of the left and right side of the human brain. The left side is analytical and verbal, the right side is instinctive and visual. So the left is labels, the right is images; grammar and vocabulary are left, but poetry comes from the right; the left is rational, but the right is relational. They argue that Jesus switches between the two in his teaching methods and operates a three-level brain of preaching. The stem of the brain is instinctive, the limbic is emotion and feeling, and the cerebrum is the thinking. They argue that we need to preach like Jesus and preach at all three levels of the brain, and that it is best to move from right to left quickly, i.e. every four to five minutes. The test of Jesus' communication and the test for any preachers today, they suggest, is 'and the common people heard him gladly'.

For those with ears to hear, the experience of youth workers involved in the educational process has a lot to teach for the benefit of the wider church.

Summary of Chapter 11

Schools are doorways to their local community. How we are involved and perceived there is a valuable learning experience for the church's wider task of being salt and light in society.

But it is in learning about learning that the church has most to benefit through its educational involvement.

While adult congregations are largely passive learners, young people are not. While adult congregations tend to be more tolerant of poor teaching, young people are not.

In the severity of the challenge of teaching today's young people lies its value.

It forces us to think again about the purpose and process of what we are trying to do and drives us to learn, both from educational theory and supremely from the perfect Teacher himself.

The lessons found here are sure to be of benefit to the whole congregation, not just young people.

12

Missionary Essentials (1)

'Christians working among the young therefore face in principle the same issues that any missionary faces when going into another culture; questions of language, custom, attitudes, values and ideas are all put into the melting pot.'[1]

For a number of years, youth workers have been looking to the missionary writers for insights and advice in communicating the gospel across cultures. In fact, 'youth missionary' is becoming an in phrase.

Increasingly today, however, there is a widespread understanding that *all* church leaders, not just youth workers, have to communicate across cultures to be effective. Here lies perhaps the greatest value of youth work to the contemporary church in today's world. Youth work trains us to think like missionaries.

Throughout the next two chapters I tend to use 'missionary' as a very general term. Of course, you can't possibly lump several hundred years of history across seven continents of the world with a variety of diverse views and approaches (let alone theologies) under one label, but because there is not the space for a variety of views on each issue, I have generalised.

OUT OF THE FRYING PAN INTO THE YOUTH CLUB...

I realised that here on the home front, I had left behind me one of the most exotic tribes of all – the young people of America. They have their own form of dress, symbolised by their omnipresent blue jeans; their own food, not always the most nutritious; their own music, which I confess, I do not understand; their own rituals, enacted as they listen to their music in concert; their own language, their own values, remarkably similar from New York to California. Dress, food, music, ritual, language, values – these are the things that make up a tribe, or a sub-culture, as they have been called. It is to that tribe, as they are, that the gospel must be brought.[2]

Christianity – a threat to culture?

More times than I care to remember as a youth worker, what I wanted to say never got heard, simply because who I was and what I had to say were perceived to be a threat to the peer group's way of living.

I will never forget one particular Boys' Brigade summer camp at which I was asked to speak. The first night, despite my best efforts, I could hardly even get their attention. The message to me was clear: they were at camp to have a good laugh, and the evening talk did not fit in with that agenda.

As I went to bed that night I could see that radical measures were called for, so at 1 am, without the knowledge of the senior officers, I approached the two oldest lads' tents and enquired if they wanted to join me on a raiding party to the local scout camp! As you can imagine, I wasn't short of volunteers!

It was a long and hilarious night, stories of which were to become legendary and bind the group together for many years to come. Crucially, though, it completely changed the atmosphere of the camp and the lads' interest in Christianity. No longer was the Christian gospel threatening to their culture – it was actually leading the way! The very next evening they were all listening. Illustrations came thick and fast from the night before, and by the end of the week a number had moved on significantly in their relationship with Christ. In missiological terms, the gospel had been heard on its own merits once it was understood that it did not constitute a threat to the culture of the lads concerned.

So much of what is misunderstood and frowned upon by the wider church as 'frivolous' youth work actually is missiologically justifiable. It is part of

SO-CALLED 'FRIVOLOUS' YOUTH WORK
IS MISSIOLOGICALLY JUSTIFIABLE...

establishing the gospel without the adult world's trappings. Sadly, though, it is not until you are identifying with youth culture that you can actually see the need for it, and the tragic result is that many youth workers are viewed as unspiritual or shallow (or with just plain bewilderment and misunderstanding!)

by their congregations, simply because the church has failed to learn from the missionaries. The truth is that the gospel needs to be placed in a context appropriate to someone's culture, and in youth work that often means raw energy and fun. So often it is not the youth worker who is shallow; it is the wider church because it has simply not thought the issue through. Tragically as a result many a youth worker today senses the same loneliness and isolation that the missionary knows only too well. In seeking to reach a particular group they get caught between two cultures and can find themselves truly at home in neither.

Again the parallels are obvious for the wider church. Christianity's general failure to engage the working classes is a case in point. It is well documented that faced with the reading, diary-administered formal relationships and smartly dressed culture of the predominantly middle-class church, working people tend to feel threatened and alienated and so stay away. Ministry groups like those working with travellers or athletes, though, have learned to organise the church experience in culturally appropriate ways and in doing so point the way forward for the whole of the church in the West today. We have to learn to bring the good news of Jesus to people without inadvertently threatening their culture.

Drawing the line

But when does not threatening a culture unconsciously cross over the line and become a compromise of Christian truth? For those willing to learn, the missionary writers teach us the principle of balance – on the one hand Jesus challenges and reveals sin in every culture, but on the other hand there are aspects of culture which are not incompatible with the lordship of Christ and therefore need not be discarded, but rather preserved and transformed.

In practice, however, missionaries have found that this is even more complicated than it sounds! Take polygamy, for example. Missionaries attempting to disciple new converts understandably took the view that polygamy was not Christian, but they made the mistake of insisting that new converts who already had more than one wife kept only one following their conversion to Christ. After watching the social havoc this wreaked in villages and the ostracising from society of many of the new converts, some missionaries began to seek out another approach. They argued that Christians witness through two basic relationships, church and family, and that culturally appropriate forms of both must be kept as a priority if evangelism is to be taken seriously. This did not mean that polygamy became acceptable, but rather that it was allowed for that generation, hoping that faith would bring about change in the culture over time.

There was the added problem too when it was found that a bad custom could nevertheless have a constructive function within that culture. So, for example, some of the ways that tribes initiated young people to adulthood may well have been cruel and/or immoral, but a clear rite of passage to adulthood was nevertheless important for people. Missionaries found that it was a mistake to stop a custom without at least providing an alternative for the function it provided to the society.

'We did not want the fact that someone was smoking cannabis to be a barrier to him getting to know God. Cannabis was not a salvation issue. If we had told the young people that they could not smoke or drink when they had come into church, then they would not have come at all.'[3]

Here lies the missiological background to the value calls that youth workers are having to make every day in what is acceptable and what needs to be challenged in youth culture.

And it is no less complicated working with teenagers than working with a two thirds world culture. For example, try to divide up the list below into three categories: what always has to stop when some teenagers become Christians; what can be allowed to continue for a time; and what can be affirmed in youth culture.

- Smoking
- Wearing fashionable clothes
- Soft drugs
- Gang membership
- Importance of friends
- Membership of sports team
- Casual sex
- Sleeping with a regular partner
- Obsessive following of a particular band/singer
- Shoplifting
- Swearing
- Skipping school

- Being rude to parents
- Drinking alcohol under age
- Watching 18-rated videos

Wider application

This very issue has made headlines in the wider church over the last year when 'living in sin' was at last officially dropped from the Church of England's language. Of course, theologically speaking, the phrase was always inappropriate (the whole world lives in sin), but the headline signalled an important process of change as the church rethinks the realities of engaging the modern world. Slowly the church is coming to see that Christian morality is not a barrier that stops people coming to Christ, but rather the Maker's instructions for life as he always intended it to be.

As we can see from the table on the next page various models of how the gospel's implications would work out in a given society have been put forward, but at the end of the day the missionaries' lesson for all to hear is that it is only after truly identifying with and appreciating a culture over a sustained period of time that we are able, under God, to make the necessary distinctions required for truly relevant and engaging faith.

A gospel that people can understand

'We will make mistakes in the process of contextualisation, but there is no mistake worse than not trying at all.'[4]

Level	Description	Example
1	Immediately renounced	Idolatry, witchcraft, sorcery, cannibalism, head-hunting, widow-strangling, infanticide, blood feuds, ritual prostitution.
2	Tolerated initially, but gradually disappear	Polygamy, caste system, slavery.
3	Churches divided on whether level 2 or level 4	Marriage practice and initiation rites.
4	Indifferent matters	Eating and bathing customs, ways of greeting the opposite sex, hair and dress styles, music.

One of the ideas the missionaries teach us in 'beginning where people are', is to find stories and images in the culture which carry within them elements and values of the gospel. These then act as bridges of understanding for the people whom the missionary is trying to reach. Missionary writers refer to them as 'redemptive analogies'.

Dr Peter Cotterell talks of his work with one of the tribes in Ethiopia where there was a traditional belief in a god whose name when literally translated meant 'the far off god'. He wisely chose this name to explain the incarnation in Amharic and was effectively saying, 'The god who was once far off has now come near.'

In the dramatic book *Bruchko*, Bruce Olson recounts his life among the Motilone tribe of Colombia. After five years of enduring a great deal of suffering he heard of a Motilone legend about a man who became an ant. 'As the story flashed into my mind, for the first time I realised its lesson. If you are big and powerful, you have to become small and weak in order to work with other weak beings. It was a perfect parallel for what God had done in Jesus.' Olson took the word for becoming like an ant and used it for the incarnation. The idea that God became a man 'stunned them'.[5]

Vincent Donovan nearly despaired of his attempts to communicate Jesus to the Masai, because much of the cultural setting of the New Testament itself was entirely alien to the Masai people. Slowly, though, glimmers of light appeared. Donovan discovered, for example, that there were in Masai culture rituals for forgiveness which effectively acted as sacraments to the people. If a son offended his father, it was usually unforgivable, but there was provision among them that spittle could be used as a sign of forgiveness. Spittle was obviously a powerful symbol of life in a dry and parched land, and the father would spit upon the son as a sign of a fresh start for their relationship. Donovan was further encouraged that divided families could be reconciled by the exchanging of food in a special meal. Both of these Masai rituals provided for Donovan the doorways to understanding that he had been searching for.

However, such an approach is obviously fraught with problems. In India, for example, some Christians took the risk of borrowing the word 'avatar' to describe the incarnation of Christ. Despite careful explanations, many Indian Christians refused to use the phrase, as it was originally borrowed from Hinduism and the so-called incarnations of Vishnu. Without great care, redemptive analogies, far from clarifying the gospel message, can actually confuse it.[6]

Don Richardson, in his contemporary missions

classic *Peace Child*, describes his frustrations in trying to communicate the gospel to head-hunting Sawi peoples of Papua New Guinea:

> For the Sawi tribe, treachery was the highest virtue, their heroes had all committed great acts of betrayal leading to the slaughter of their 'friends'. To them, Judas was seen as a wonderful hero of treachery. How could they respond to Jesus?
>
> The breakthrough came with an even more powerful story in their own legends of 'the peace child'. Peace could be made by offering one's own child to deadly enemies. God's love in giving his own 'Peace Child' communicated – and many of these cannibalistic peoples have since come to Christ.[7]

Many missiologists believe that God has placed such imagery in every culture.

Redemptive analogies in youth culture

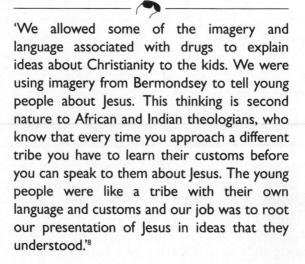

'We allowed some of the imagery and language associated with drugs to explain ideas about Christianity to the kids. We were using imagery from Bermondsey to tell young people about Jesus. This thinking is second nature to African and Indian theologians, who know that every time you approach a different tribe you have to learn their customs before you can speak to them about Jesus. The young people were like a tribe with their own language and customs and our job was to root our presentation of Jesus in ideas that they understood.'[8]

In such a vastly different type of cultural setting, the redemptive analogies in the world of today's young people take a very different form. In a culture dominated by the media, it is inevitably the media, especially through films, soaps, music and news stories, which provide the bridges of under-standing into which the work of Christ can be understood today.

Instructor saved Briton in 6,000 ft fall

A British skydiver who survived a 6,000 ft fall when his parachute failed to open was probably saved by the sacrifice of the instructor who fell with him.[9]

There are, of course, opportunities other than redemptive analogies which present doorways of understanding for the gospel in today's culture. While they may not capture the heart of the gospel message like a redemptive analogy does, they can nevertheless be very valuable 'windows' for understanding. Into this category regularly come lines from songs in the charts, quotes from media stars, story lines from the soaps, etc.

This is not to say, of course, that the media provide the only form of helping the gospel message connect with young people. As we have already seen, the model of Jesus' teaching is very interactive and informal, so family and peer group experiences and the 'hot issues of the moment' for a group of young people are all excellent opportunities.

I once had two very troubled lads in the back of the car as I approached a roundabout. Braking in the normal way, I was hit from behind by another driver who was simply going too fast. Having checked that the lads were OK, I got out and went to have a word with the offending driver! As I did so, I saw out of the corner of my eye that the two lads had unstrapped their belts, wound down the window and were, for once in their lives, giving me their undivided attention! It struck me that whatever I was to say in the future about handling personal anger, this would be the lesson they would remember! I found the thought a most calming one and the journey home was a once-in-a-lifetime opportunity to really connect with two angry young men about coping with the way they were feeling inside.

FOR ONCE IN THEIR LIVES THE TWO LADS WERE NOW GIVING ME THEIR UNDIVIDED ATTENTION...

A church people can relate to

Once the gospel is being understood, the highest priority for the missionary is to establish a church in which indigenous people feel comfortable; where they can celebrate and learn more about their faith in their own culture. Why? Because worship must be genuine and sincere and this is more likely (though never guaranteed) when church practice is relevant to the culture. Relevance is only a means to an end though, as it is authenticity which is our goal. For this to happen effectively, it is widely recognised that a number of things are important, from the design of the building to the style of dress; from the atmosphere of the meeting to its length; from the style of the teaching to the amount of participation by the congregation and so on.

In his book *Bread of Life*, Ron Sider uses the example of the church in Bali as a leading example of a church truly relevant to its people.

Even in 1971, every aspect of the Bali church – its architecture, music and worship – was Western. So much so that Bali Christians were sick of the label 'Black Dutch'. They wanted to end their isolation from Bali culture, so in 1972 Dr Wayan Mastra chaired a watershed synod of the Bali Christians. They built a cultural training centre called a temple of meditation, which would use Balinese architecture and art to proclaim the gospel in ways relevant to the Bali people, 'to help Balinese Christians gain a greater appreciation of their cultural heritage within the context of their faith and to find new ways of expressing that faith within the culture'.[10] The Bali church also recognised that Bali culture is very visual and that words are not enough, so they set about an ambitious programme of social action to demonstrate visually their proclamation of the kingdom of God.

Of all the issues related to contextualised church, though, the singularly most influential factor that missionaries have found in establishing the cultural fit of a church is the style of the music used. Here lies a hard challenge for today's church.

Contemporary church faces the music

'The Church must celebrate, sing and dance the gospel in its own cultural medium.'[11]

When I started working as a youth minister twelve years ago, I was part of a vibrant local church which would best be described as 'renewed evangelical'. At that time, non-Christian teenagers whom we were contacting through schools and clubs were interested by church and often enjoyed attending, particularly the evening service. Ten years later, however, despite many improvements in the way the church did things, the evening service was more than many of the Christian teenagers could tolerate, let alone the non-Christians. Culture had changed that rapidly.

Even for teenagers from Christian families, much of what went on was out of tune with their world. To the average member of the congregation, this was incomprehensible. We had moved with the times: we no longer had pews or pulpits, a band had replaced the keyboard, women often led and we even had a video screen and projector. Compared with other churches we were positively trendy! Surely we were more in tune with youth culture now than we ever were? The truth was that we had copied the effect but missed the heart of a changing culture.

A defining moment for me came with the arrival on the wider Christian scene of two young and very gifted new worship leaders, Martin Smith and Matt Redman. As Elvis had done in the 1950s for a previous generation of disenfranchised young people, so Smith and Redman now gave a voice to post-modern people feeling trapped in a modernist church.

Smith and Redman were the first generation of worship leaders not to have grown up in a hymn culture and consequently their music more naturally reflected a mainstream chart sound. It was not possible to lead this kind of music from a piano or organ, it was a style largely alien to the majority of classically trained musicians and it was loud!

Their impact, though, was not just one of style; it was one of substance too. There was a significant shift in the lyrical content of the songs. They dropped much of the well-worn biblical language, familiar both in hymns and modern songs, and allowed the message to become more oblique and at times deliberately vague. They also included a massive injection of hope, anticipation and longing for renewal and revival. Meaning came through pictures more than principle, and above all the music was passionate.

It was the arrival of this music which clearly revealed to me the entrapment of even renewed evangelicalism within modernist culture. Introducing the songs into church was fascinating.

For some, here was music which at last gave vent to so much of what they felt in a natural musical form. Here were words that didn't try to box God in and here was music that you could really dance to. For the majority of my brothers and sisters in Christ, though, here was a tune they couldn't get, to words they didn't understand, in a style that they just didn't like!

I began to see that for all the inspiration of Graham Kendrick's work, that which is most used in churches is basically a hymn style musically and an objective message lyrically. That is not intended to be in any way critical of Kendrick, who will go down in church history as one of the great hymn writers. It is simply to recognise that times are once again changing. New styles of Christian music are necessary to engage even an increasing number of Christians, let alone non-Christians, in today's world. Just as William Booth in the nineteenth century was driven to use the melodies of the music hall to make Christian worship comprehensible for those he worked with in the inner city, so now new writers and worship leaders will use styles and images that make Christian worship comprehensible to contemporary youth culture.

We must, of course, recognise that no one musical style will reach even a majority these days. Neither do I want to suggest for one moment a hint of confrontation to music that was penned from young men who have a passion for unity, nor suggest that changes to our worship patterns should happen uncritically. Nevertheless, there is a sense of a day of reckoning arriving for the generation of evangelical leaders who emerged in the seventies and early eighties. Did they win through the reforms to traditional church in the sixties and seventies to engage a lost world, or did they really do it because they personally preferred it? Perhaps their response to this new music and the movement that goes with it will actually tell us all the answer.

'The traditional church are truly God's people, but my heart is for the 90 per cent of this world who will not traditionalise in order to become Christian.'[12]

Perhaps the most famous contemporary church is Willow Creek in the United States. Steve Gerali, who was on the staff there, wrote this: 'The contemporary church now sits in the seat of the traditional church and forgets its heritage and the process of contextualisation that shaped its success.'[13]

Still deeper to go

Most worrying of all is what the missionaries were to discover next. After all the struggles of learning to draw the line and not unnecessarily threaten culture; after all the hard work of attempting to contextualise both the gospel and ways of doing church, they found there was still deeper to go. The simple discovery was this: a contextualised gospel message engaged people's minds, and a contextualised church engaged people's emotions, but it took more than that to capture the soul of the people's culture.

Take, for example, Africa. It could be said that a lot of progress has been made in engaging indigenous people with culturally appropriate forms of worship.[14] Proverbs and stories are used in preaching, which encourage oral responses from the congregation. Liturgical dance, based on traditional dances, is used and church music is based on traditional patterns, with active participation by the congregation.

But even here, there is something missing. The key moments of human life – those most important to all of us like birth, marriage, death and burial – are often still marked in two separate ways and in two different places by African Christians. First there is the traditional tribal manner and then there is the 'Christian way', with little interaction or integration between the two. In other words, the gospel is not allowed to fully shape the life of the people. The soul of culture still evades the gospel.

Such a discovery was to have huge implications for the mission movement, many of which are still being grappled with today. Faced with the harsh reality that even after contextualising the gospel message and church methods, Christianity was still being tacked on to culture rather than transforming it, the missionary thinkers were forced back to the very core issues of their enterprise. What they were to discover we look at in the next chapter.

Summary of Chapter 12

Virtually all evangelism today is cross-cultural.

One of the essential contributions that youth work brings to the church is to teach us that we must learn from missionaries if we are to communicate successfully.

In particular we must learn:

- not to inadvertently threaten someone's culture by what we present of the church;
- where to draw the line in the engagement between the gospel and a culture;
- to communicate a message that people can understand;
- a church practice that they can relate to.

Most important of all, though, we must learn that all this is *still not enough*.

13

Missionary Essentials (2)

God does not want us to be instant cross cultural experts. He does however want us to begin changing.[1]

Missionary influence

It is worth noting at the start of this chapter that a number of nationwide initiatives for the wider church over the last few years have drawn heavily on missionary teaching and experience.

Missionary Congregations, for example, is a mainly Anglican movement, led by Robert Warren, the Archbishop's Special Advisor for Evangelism. With the mottoes of 'Reaching more by doing less!' and 'Being a different kind of church', its whole philosophy is very closely mission linked.

The Willow Creek Church has been hugely influential in this country over recent years, with a very carefully focused mission-based strategy for the local community. Similarly, Laurence Singlehurst of YWAM has, in his book *Sowing, Reaping, Keeping*, clearly articulated a mission strategy as foundational for the church in our post-Christian society. It is exciting to see these mission themes being taken up and applied to the local church context.

Perhaps the singularly most exciting and releasing initiative for the wider church in recent years, though, has been the Alpha course. Massively popular across a broad spectrum of denominations, Alpha has succeeded in marrying the climate of the age with the traditional message of Christ. As a result, thousands have come to faith. Once again, there are a number of themes central to the ethos of Alpha which are hard-learned lessons from the missionaries. Understanding that conversion is often a process rather than an event[2], and using inclusive phrases like 'spiritual journey' to encompass this. The emphasis on open discussion and free expression are the refined lessons of dialogue, honed over the years by the missionaries. Even the emphasis on the work of the Holy Spirit can be seen to recapture the two thirds world emphasis that Christ is to be experienced as well as understood.

However, we must be careful! Once again in church history we are in danger of copying the effect and yet losing the heart of what we are trying to accomplish. As we saw in the last chapter, the missionaries found that even after contextualising the gospel and ways of doing church, it was still not enough to really capture the heart and soul of people.

Isn't that precisely the situation we find ourselves in today? For all our efforts in reforming our ecclesiology and rethinking our proclamation, as we saw in Chapter 2 Christianity is still caught up in Western culture with a privately engaging but publicly irrelevant faith. Capturing the heart and soul of a people's culture is in no way just a two thirds world issue. It affects you and me.

If our goal is that the whole of life is orientated

towards God; if our goal is that the church has no walls to the community, the missionary writers teach us that there is still further to go if we really mean business.

To capture the soul of a culture we first need to go back to the beginning. We need to ask the fundamental questions as the missionaries did about who we are and what we are trying to do.

What is the purpose of mission?

The great missionary writer, Roland Allen, has been described as a lonely prophet. Writing at the turn of the century based on his experiences in China, his work was always ahead of his time. He argued passionately and strongly that the only way to see a truly at-home and life-engaging expression of Christianity in a culture was for the church to be led from the very start by the people themselves.

> If the first converts are taught to depend upon the missionary, if all work is concentrated in his hands, the community learns to rest passively upon the man from whom they receive their first insight into the gospel. Paul founded churches, we found missions.[3]

In his provocative book *Missionary Methods – St Paul's or Ours?*, Allen went against the accepted thinking of his day and challenged the missionary movement to take more seriously the church-planting model of the apostle Paul. The Spirit of Christ is the spirit of initiative. Nothing comes near to Paul when he preached the gospel not the law and then retired from his converts to give place to Christ. To do this, he had the spirit of faith. He was persuaded that the Spirit of Christ would teach them to approve that example and inspire them to follow it. He trusted his converts because he believed in the spirit within them.

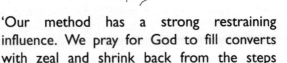

'Our method has a strong restraining influence. We pray for God to fill converts with zeal and shrink back from the steps which would encourage this.'[4]

The purpose of mission was being redefined. Instead of establishing a church for a group of people, mission was to focus on evangelism and leadership support. The young church could then naturally grow up among the new indigenous converts. Without this responsibility for the future of Christianity in their world, Allen believed that the gospel would never capture the soul of a culture.

The role of the missionary

As the purpose of mission was changing, so the role of the missionary had to change too.

Vincent Donovan was a Catholic missionary influenced by Allen's work, who worked with the famous Masai tribe of Kenya in the 1960s. In his well-known book *Christianity Rediscovered*, Donovan wrote of this process of re-evaluating his missionary role as he tried to discover how to evangelise this formidable tribe.

It is almost as if the authors of the mission wish upon the third world church all the ills of western institutionalism. We build a 100 year strategy when what we want to do is not stay longer than necessary. We tend to feel that we need to leave them with an institution before we go. Instead we must leave them with what Paul did. The gospel is the affair of the missionary. Interpretation of the gospel is the affair of the people.

I would propose cutting myself off from the schools and the hospital and just go and talk to them about God and the Christian message. I have no theory, no plan, no strategy, no gimmicks, no idea of what will come. I feel rather naked. I will begin as soon as possible.[5]

Donovan set about his task:

I then pointed out that we were well known among the Masai for our work in schools and hospitals and for our interest in Maṣai and their cattle. But now I no longer wanted to talk about schools and hospitals, but about God in the life of the Masai and about the message of Christianity. Indeed it was for this very work that I came here from far away.

Ndangoya looked at me for a long time and then said in a puzzled way, 'If that is why you came here, why did you wait so long to tell us about this?'[6]

'As a missionary in South India, the most basic idea that I had drummed in to me was the idea that no-one should impose an interpretation of Christianity on anybody else, but instead people should be allowed to develop their own understanding of God... Ten years after coming back from India, I was learning to apply the same missionary critique to work in my own country, in Bermondsey.'[7]

Institutionalism

It is worth noting too that pioneering missionaries like Donovan and Allen felt great frustration with the institutional approach of the missionary movement. They found there was no room for direct evangelism and had to ignore the system to conduct it. They were, in effect, highly disruptive. Of course, in doing so they were actually drawing the mission back to its reason for its existence, its true heart.

'I had to plant the seed of the gospel in the Masai culture and let it grow wild.'[8]

Similarly today, young people's work is notorious for not fitting in with the traditional way the church goes about things. Once again we must learn the lessons of the missionary. We must learn that youth workers, far from being disruptive, are actually calling the church back to its true mission. We have to see our structures as a means to an end, not an end in themselves.

'Our organisation immobilises our missionaries. It creates and maintains large stations and great institutions and these absorb a very great proportion of our energy. We cannot move freely.'[9]

Participation in mission

We have done everything for them except acknowledge their equality. We have done everything for them, but very little with them. We have done everything for them except give place to them. We have treated them as dear children, but not as brethren.[10]

This change of role for the missionary led to a far greater emphasis on participation by indigenous people in mission activity.

Bishop Lesslie Newbigin writes powerfully of the value of this kind of participation. During his time as Bishop in India he resolutely refused umpteen requests to send missionaries to support young converts in villages throughout his area. Instead he sent trained Indian helpers to advise and support, so that the fledgling church learned right from the start not to be dependent on the mission for its existence. A few years later there was a resurgence of militant Hinduism in the area and all the new churches were approached to renounce their Christian faith. Only one did, and it was the one church to whom a missionary had been sent.

The lesson of the missionaries is that patterns of doing church cannot be imposed upon people of a different culture, but must be entrusted to the Spirit at work in young converts' lives. Worship, leadership and church practice must flow out of the trial and error of the fledgling church interpreting God's word for themselves if that church is to be truly evangelistic and an engaging expression of the Christian gospel to the people of that culture.

These missionaries teach us that leadership is better grown from within than imposed from outside. Not only does this have profound implications for the selection and allocation process of most of the denominations today, but significantly it has a great deal to say about the nature of church leadership in a changing world.

Application for today

Not that we should be uncritical of missionary teaching, of course. First it must be evaluated against the Bible's teaching and then against our own experience. We must also be mindful of a different cultural setting. For all the hardship and loneliness that these missionaries endured, I can't help feeling just a little envious of some of them. After all, they had one defined and stable culture to reach with the gospel. The task of the church in today's Western world is more complicated and involved. Cultural engagement, it seems, involves aiming at a constantly moving target!

For all that, though, there is no doubt in my mind that it is at this point that missionary insights are of perhaps the greatest value to the contemporary church. For all our talk of releasing and equipping the laity, we have actually missed the point.

By the time we release people into church leadership they are already subtly indoctrinated into a church way of doing things. In effect we are not really letting go, merely tinkering with what is already there. The more biblical model rediscovered by the likes of Allen and Donovan is that this delegation of responsibility must start from day one if the church is ever going to have the fresh cultural cutting edge we all long for, although we must of course hold Paul's model of church planting in tension with his counsel in 1 Timothy 5:22 not to be hasty in setting aside people for leadership.

A great window of opportunity to explore this issue

more thoroughly is provided for the church today through its work with young people. It is, however, a window that has in some quarters got off to a difficult start.

NOW THE STEWARDS WILL WAIT UPON US FOR TONIGHT'S OFFERING...

BY THE TIME WE RELEASE PEOPLE INTO CHURCH LEADERSHIP THEY ARE ALREADY INDOCTRINATED INTO A 'CHURCHY' WAY OF DOING THINGS...

Youth congregations

A youth congregation is not to be confused with a youth church. A youth church is fully autonomous, whereas a youth congregation, while normally meeting separately from the adult church, comes under that church's leadership authority.

There are currently a growing number of experiments with youth congregations, and their very existence has been more than a little controversial, as the furore surrounding the Nine O' Clock Service in Sheffield has shown. The debate has even managed to bring into the open disagreement between the current

Archbishop of Canterbury and his predecessor! So what should our response be to youth congregations?

> 'Perhaps the days of immediately incorporating young people into our existing church structures are over.'[11]

ARGUMENTS AGAINST YOUTH CONGREGATIONS

Opponents of youth congregations would cite a number of arguments to support their view.

They are unbiblical

Authors like Donald McGavron would suggest that church growth in the book of Acts is never limited to a particular group, but includes all people groups. In fact, Gordon Fee is quoted as saying that homogenous (or same people type) congregations have no biblical foundation.[12]

They misrepresent the gospel

Paul makes it so abundantly clear that the nature of church is to model a supernatural oneness to a fragmented world, that to have separate services for young people is a denial of one of the basic gospel principles.

They are illogical

The argument goes that if the church is failing, it is the church that must be changed. It is illogical to set up alternatives.

They short change teenagers

Most teenagers want to relate to, and be accepted by,

adults. If we encourage youth congregations, we take away that opportunity, at least within the church family.

They ignore church history

Michael Harper makes the point (though not about youth congregations per se) that when groups separate from organisations out of tension with the old, they subconsciously plan a corrective which then successive generations of the movement immediately make normative! In other words, reactions against something always tend to react too far and need to be brought back again.

They are an extension of a failed method

Most youth congregations are really glorified youth groups in disguise! Not a lot has changed in their foundational thinking, merely the trappings and the title! It is still basically a halfway house approach. The teenagers cannot cope with church right now, so the thinking goes that we will try to hold on to them for a few years and hopefully they will integrate with the wider church a number of years down the line. We have to be bold enough to see that this approach has not worked for the last thirty years, so it is hardly likely to get much better in the future, even if we do call it by a new name!

They are simplistic

A youth congregation cannot work, simply because youth culture has separated into so many tribes anyway that what appeals to one will only alienate another, thus perpetuating the problem of failing to truly engage people where they are.

They lack experience and wisdom

Pastoral care and counselling are part of normal church life, but if a congregation is going to be made up of only young people, there will be a lack of those with enough life experience and situational stability to support people in need. There is the added problem that with only a few adult leaders around, this can give those leaders an undue influence, which can be unhealthy.

They make the generation gap worse

Far from encouraging unity, youth congregations may only heighten the generational tensions between God's people.

They have no future

Youth congregations inevitably grow older. Faced with this, what is their long-term purpose?

Take all of the above at face value and it would appear that youth congregations are at best a colossal waste of time and effort, and at worst a strategy straight from hell! By turning to the missionaries, though, the above is put in a different perspective.

First we have to try to understand why the need for youth congregations has arisen in the first place.

'The clear though underlying objective of much church youth work is to keep adults happy.'[13]

'Churches want young people like warders want prisoners – for the roll call.'[14]

REASONS FOR YOUTH CONGREGATIONS

- A growing number of Christians wanting to follow Jesus, but finding the church culturally alienating.
- Many young people in the church already feeling powerless and frustrated by their lack of leadership opportunity.
- A sense of rejection from organised Christianity for those who don't quite fit into middle-class society.
- The failure of the church to disciple and pastor young people in their own culture.
- To harness the potential of modern media and technology in church communication.
- Youth leaders reaching the point of exasperation with the established church and wanting to do something new.

FROM A MISSIONARY PERSPECTIVE

As soon as we start thinking about the issue, a missionary perspective immediately recognises that evangelism and discipleship in a person's culture are crucially important if the gospel's implications are ever to truly impact society.

What is currently allowed to go on in today's churches is tragic. Most young people in Britain today never genuinely hear the gospel. Those who do, reject it because they perceive their culture to be threatened by all the trappings of the church. For the tiny minority of young people who do respond to Christ, they are caught between the two worlds of church and culture, and a privately engaging but publicly irrelevant faith is often the result.

As we have seen, the only way that the missionaries have found to combat this problem is to allow the converts to shape their own church, to give them the freedom of cultural expression and autonomous leadership. The gospel is the affair of the missionary, the church is the affair of the people.

This is the truly biblical way of dealing with conversion to Christ in a culture different from our own. Fee's point is misleading. It is true that youth congregations (and homogenous congregations in general) have no *explicit* biblical foundation, but then neither do the sermon and the worship time that are so much part of our church life. It is an argument from silence. The truth is that the book of Acts does not give us a detailed breakdown of the make-up and practice of those early house churches. When one takes on board all the Bible's teaching on culture, to say that youth congregations have no biblical foundation is misleading.

'To the weak I became weak, to win the weak. I have become all things to all men so that by all possible means I might save some' (1 Cor 9:22).

The argument that youth congregations ignore the lessons of history is selective at best. We will look at young people in church history in the last chapter, but simply note at this point that evangelical renewal has often gone hand in hand with the harnessing of new technology. Luther and the printing press, Booth and the 'music hall approach' for industrial Britain, even Billy Graham and the evangelistic rallies (with all the PA and advertising technology they required) are cases in point. Most youth congregations are trying to harness new forms of technology to communicate with the next generation. In doing so, they follow a fine tradition.

All of the previous objections to youth congregations, however, cannot be ignored. They have to be addressed if the congregations are to continue. Ultimately it comes down to three things: the way the congregation is established, the relationship it has with the wider church, and the leadership structure. If the mission writers were to be heeded properly at these three crucial points, it would make a tremendous impact. I believe a number of things would happen.

First, youth congregations would not be called youth congregations! They would not be trying to reach all young people or stay forever youthful. The issue is one of culture, not age. The task is to sow the seed of the gospel in the non-church culture of new converts and let it grow beyond that generation and beyond the patterns of established church (with no expectation that one day it should come back to look like it either!). It is the responsibility of the new converts together to live and act as the bride of Christ in their culture.

Congregations would not be set up by frustrated young people and youth leaders reacting against the church. Rather they would be encouraged and nurtured by church leaders themselves as a development of the church's ministry. Of crucial importance is that the congregation remain under the pastoral care, teaching and oversight of the church. Heather Evans makes this point, quoting Priest, a missionary who many years later followed Donovan to work with the Kenyan Masai, only to make a sad discovery: 'While Donovan's approach was commendable, in personal visits in the area several years after he left, I was saddened to learn that most all of the new believers had not continued in relation to the church, *due to a lack of continued teaching.*'[15]

This continued teaching is the biblical model. That is the reason for most of the New Testament letters. The churches Paul planted were autonomous and truly indigenous, but they were not simply left on their own to get on with it. They were overseen and supported, challenged and corrected, resourced with both people and teaching. If this relationship were to be recreated today at the local level with so called 'youth' congregations, all the previous objections would be dealt with.

The role of those directly involved in the oversight of the congregation becomes the role of the missionary that writers like Donovan, Newbigin and Allen have defined: encouraging indigenous leadership at every level and allowing the congregation to apply biblical principles in forms culturally appropriate to themselves.

There is no doubt that we are best together, but there is no reason why worshipping in different ways should bring division. With wise oversight the new congregation is free to enjoy a more equal and meaningful sense of unity with brothers and sisters in the adult church, with arranged opportunities to work and pray, fellowship and worship together.

From a missionary perspective, a church that meets in more than one congregation and takes the unique oneness of the body of Christ seriously is both a logical and biblical way forward for the church in the Western world today.

'The future agenda for those working with young people it seems will increasingly focus on developing patterns of church life which are able to embrace cultural change and diversity whilst maintaining a gospel commitment to the unity of the church.'[16]

I, for one, have concerns about some current youth congregations, in particular their pastoral oversight and biblical teaching, as well as their long-term strategy. However, it seems clear that rather than standing on the margins, watching and almost waiting for them to fail, every effort should be made to put missionary church planters and youth workers together, lest we miss out on a God-given opportunity for the church in this country truly to engage with our culture, perhaps like never before.

'Alternative worship is a phenomenon which almost invites misunderstanding. There is considerable technological complexity sitting alongside simplicity and directness. The movement among young people to express worship in church life within the frameworks of popular culture is both profound and strategic.'[17]

I truly believe that if we would only take the lessons of the missionaries seriously, it would lead to a radical reappraisal of our traditional patterns of church leadership, help us to rediscover a far more robust, practical and participatory missionary model of church, and help us to understand so-called youth congregations not as a threat but more as an opportunity for the church to break free in our contemporary world today.

Summary of Chapter 13

Contemporary church is influenced by missionary thinking – but not enough.

When missionary influence goes no deeper than a message people can understand with a way of doing church that they can relate to, the basic problems of the church's culture traps are unlikely to be resolved.

If, however, we learn with the great mission thinkers to re-evaluate our role in mission, the place of the institution in mission and, most of all, the potential of new converts to be God's church in their own culture, then things could be very different.

The essential value of youth work in all this is that the contentious issue of youth congregations requires us to respond to all these issues now.

I4

Leadership Essentials

Church youth work has big implications for Christian leadership, partly because it tends to act like a trigger for issues crucial to the health and well-being of the whole congregation. In the first part of the chapter we look at some of these.

But perhaps the greatest leadership significance for church youth work is that it has been a powerful formative influence in making the whole church what it is today. If that is the case the great leadership opportunity is that we can, under God, change the future by working with young people now. We look at this in the second part of the chapter.

PART 1

Keeping contemporary

As we saw in Section Two, youthism – a focus by the media on all things young – has a major effect on society. The colossal amount of time, energy, money and resources spent both appealing to and appearing as young, shapes our culture's values, our goals of who we want to be and the lifestyle we want to lead. It is not an overstatement to say that nowadays popular culture is largely youth driven.

Take the Spice Girls, for example. Originally re-cruited, rehearsed and packaged for the young teen market, they have grown into a cultural phenomenon. They have 'conquered' America, sold more records than any other female band in history and have had six successive number one hits (not bad for a band that generally doesn't sing live!).

The fashion spin-offs have been immense and Spice Girls bric-à-brac and memorabilia are everywhere. Popular image brings with it a popular message – Girl Power! Sexy assertiveness and disrespect for the establishment is most definitely a defining cultural statement for many more than merely the youngest of teenage girls.

What is the importance of all this for the church? It is best summed up by American pastor Leith Anderson, author of a number of books on church leadership: 'Those who do not keep up with what is happening with children and adolescents are in danger of being out of touch within twenty-four months.'[1]

It seems the church is always trying to catch up with cultural change. Working closely with young people will help the church *keep ahead*, not just *keep up*.

Church growth

Evangelicalism in the United States supports an industry of consultants, advisors, commentators and analysts. For all its excesses, there is little doubt that in its depth and breadth of analysis in church trends, it is without parallel in the world today. For those willing to look, there is a lot to learn from the

American church growth movement.

George Barna is one of the leading lights in this industry. Based on his extensive research, he consistently argues that young people's work is crucial to the health of any church. He found that strong, healthy churches placed a high priority on youth work, while weaker ones did not. In his book *Evangelism That Works*, he argues that people go to church not for what they can contribute, but for what they can get. So it is that successful churches are providing 'valuable religious education for children of unchurched parents'.[2]

In his book *User Friendly Churches*, he even suggests that ministry to children and young people often has a more profound impact on the spiritual development of their parents than the pastor's teaching does![3] Barna's research also led him to the conclusion that youth work tends to bring a momentum and energy to a church, as well as provide a valuable testing ground for new ideas. He states: 'Ministry to children and youth is difficult in a changing world. It is also absolutely essential for long-term church growth.'[4]

Dynamism

Time and time again, youth work injects energy and momentum into the experience of the adult congregation. Often this is brought about by simple things, like a request for prayer during a youth weekend away, for example. This gives the church a fresh focus, and the encouragement that a youth service brings lifts the mood of a church. Young people taking a summer or a year out to serve God and the commissioning process that goes with it contribute to that often illusive 'feel good factor' in church life. But there are more substantial reasons too for this dynamic which youth work brings to the church.

One is creativity. The sheer ingenuity of youth, plus a natural resistance to letting the past dictate the future, means that young people and their leaders often bring a freshness and vitality to church life through creativity. From drama in services to slave auctions for the two thirds world; from evangelistic escapology to social care sleepouts; from twenty-four-hour famines to beggars' banquets; from Parable of the Talent weekends to dance and painting in worship – young people with the right encouragement bring a creative energy to church life. One of the sad things, of course, is that we should all thrive on creativity (after all, it is hereditary!) but our inbuilt adult reserve sometimes needs the justification that 'it is for the young people' for the rest of us to let our hair down and express ourselves too!

The greatest source of dynamism that youth work brings to the church, though, is conversion. Nothing is more important to Christians than seeing people come to Christ, and statistically most Christians are converted in their teenage years. Ministering to the group with the highest potential of conversion has a way of 'impacting the church environment dynamically'.[5]

Vision

Dynamism and creativity in turn help congregations to begin to map out their future. A sense of momentum brings with it a sense of anticipation for what is around the corner. It is in this atmosphere of hope and expectation that vision begins to emerge.

> 'A vision catches results in action and a congregation won't move without one.'[6]

Young people can be helpful in this vision-forming process precisely because of what we often think disqualifies them – their youthful idealism. Biblical examples of youngsters like David and Josiah show us that this is often precisely what is needed to offset the sadly too prevalent cynicism and negativism of older Christians. It is often the very fact that young people have not been alive long enough to see some of their dreams crash that makes them of special value in anticipating God's future.

Fewer and fewer youth groups these days are networking in denominational groupings. Church young people today are far more likely to go to interdenominational events like Spring Harvest rather than say a Baptist youth convention or Anglican house party. At a very practical level, it makes much more sense for youth leaders to have joint events with youth groups in the same town rather than regional or county events with the same denomination. This all promises much for the future. Instead of being caught up in parochialness, one of the exciting legacies of today's church youth work may be a generation coming through into leadership who think and work more in terms of the kingdom rather than simply the denomination.

'We cannot be the Church and cannot
confront our culture when our denominations are an inner and spiritual surrender to
the ideology of our culture.'[7]

Learning from youthful idealism

It has been noted by a number of educational
psychologists that adolescence often includes within it
an idealistic phase – a period of thought development
in which there is a very strong sense of justice and
fairness and in which many views about what is right
are shaped without the tempering of broader life
experience. In Christian teenagers this can often be
reflected in a greater measure of faith.

Many times as I have talked with young people I
have found it difficult to keep a straight face, simply
because what was being suggested was so totally
naive! However, there have been other occasions when
I have been profoundly challenged by their simple,
trusting faith.

One such occasion was the opening of our Express
Bar. The bar was an attempt to create a credible and
safe environment for teenagers to spend a Saturday
evening. It was to form the successful base of our
befriending strategy for a number of years.

Involving the youth group from its conception, we
started together to design the layout and decor. At one
of those early meetings we chose a two-tier seating
arrangement for part of the bar area, and we began
what was to become an exhausting search for the stage
blocks to make it possible. As we finished in prayer on

that first planning evening, one of the teenagers asked God to provide the stage blocks for us. It was a prayer often repeated over the next three months, as everything else (including quadraphonic sound system, a huge array of lighting, video screen and projector, not to mention a twenty-foot bar and the staff to run it) incredibly came together, but not the stage blocks. Nevertheless, despite my cautious noises to the contrary, the team took each new provision we received as confirmation that God was with us and they continued asking in faith for the stage blocks. I had exhausted every possible avenue of enquiry, only to find the prices prohibitive, but three days before we opened, a headmaster in a town twelve miles away rang me and simply said, 'You couldn't use some stage blocks, could you?' They were the ideal size and completely free. All we had to do was go and collect them. It was a huge learning experience for all of us, but I suspect especially for me!

As I reflected on it, Scripture seemed to suggest that adults must be prepared to be humble and learn from this simple uncomplicated faith. 'Young men will see visions,' says the Bible, and David, Josiah and Samuel are all excellent cases in point of a God-given, naive faith which won the day and convinced older and more cynical leaders in the process.

Technology

As steam did to the Industrial Revolution and as the motor car did to the modern road network, history teaches us that technological development eventually shapes the way we all live. The link between technical innovation and lifestyle is inescapable. It is only a matter of time before one affects the other. Today we are living through a technological revolution and the implications for the way we all live are as great as the Industrial Revolution was to rural Britain in the nineteenth century.

Despite the fact that technology is already changing the way people learn and think, for the vast majority of churches the technological revolution has simply not begun. We may have a computer in the office, but in terms of church teaching and corporate worship the technological revolution has simply passed us by.

In allowing this to happen, we have forgotten our heritage. The first apostles used the latest technology of the Roman roads to spread the gospel, and our Reformation forefathers were quick to seize on the opportunity that the printing press provided. We must do the same.

Here is another area where young people can help the church. Having grown up in the technological revolution, young people are the most at ease with its implications for the church today. Products of a multi-media world, they expect and demand multi-media communication.

While recognising that high tech is often limited by high cost, we must not simply write it off as too expensive. After all, stained-glass windows are expensive. It is all a question of priorities! We must also remind ourselves that high tech must never replace high touch relational church. Having made both these points, though, if we are truly to engage with our contemporary culture, it is important for the church to address the issue of technology.

There is a place for large video screens with gen locks to computer terminals for graphics and headline texts, as well as videos, a proper PA system for our easy listening CD culture, slide sequences, live telephone interviews and projected graphic images. With wise use all these can enhance worship in our churches today and make our services more attractive and engaging to a non-Christian society.

I can't be the only youth worker who has spent time and energy fund-raising for a large video screen for work with young people, only to find that within a year of purchase, the adult church was using it nearly as much as we were! Work with young people encourages the church to make use of modern technology.

Speaking

One of the greatest challenges to those working with young people is also one of the greatest rewards. Public speaking to groups of teenagers is hard work – school assemblies and the like are things that nightmares are made of! They demand brevity, energy, humour, story-telling from an interesting angle, variety of tone and pace and stature, just to keep young people's attention and if you don't hit the mark, they certainly let you know!

However, the benefit of communicating regularly with teenagers is that you become a better speaker. If you can hold their attention, you can hold anybody's and if you can help them understand biblical truth, you can help adults too.

PUBLIC SPEAKING TO GROUPS
OF TEENAGERS IS HARD WORK...

This discipline has left a lasting legacy in the church. There are very few of our best preachers and teachers who did not learn their trade working with young people. Mind you, it is a discipline that needs to be continued. Working with adult congregations may keep our exegesis sharp, but communication skills can easily get sloppy as adult congregations are just too nice!

PART 2

Back to the future

Just as youth work has shaped the church we have today, so what we do with young people now will shape the church we become in the future.

Pete Ward, the Archbishop of Canterbury's Special Advisor on Youth Work, has written most extensively on this subject. He argues persuasively that Anglican evangelicalism has been decisively shaped by its work among young people.

Historically, the evidence is persuasive. For example, he shows how the youth work movement CSSM, founded in 1867 (and later to become Scripture Union), was the leading light in helping define evangelical spiritual disciplines such as a daily Bible reading and quiet time and it was they who also first introduced to Christian worship the concept of the chorus. CSSM was a youth movement that as historian John Pollock has described 'slowly changed an aspect of British religion'.

Of outstanding influence on the future of evangelicalism were the CSSM camps started in the 1920s, under the leadership of Eric Nash (known as Bash). 'Bash camps' drew from élite schools and had a massive influence. Converts included John Stott, Michael Green, David Watson and Dick Lucas. Dick Lucas has made it clear that in his mind the training offered by Bash camps was far in advance of anything found in the Church of England's training colleges. By 1982, it was estimated that 7,000 boys had passed through the camps and David Watson wrote that over five years he went to no fewer than thirty-five of them!

Alister McGrath has described Bash camps as forming 'a new generation of evangelical thinkers and leaders'[8] and makes particular reference to the importance of John Stott's conversion through the camp, saying that Stott went on to be the most influential evangelical thinker of the post-war period.

Richard Bewdler, himself a graduate of the Bash camps, went on to set up Pathfinders, which has been massively influential in shaping the youth fellowship programme of most Anglican churches. There are not many Anglican clergy today who have never attended a Pathfinder or CYFA camp or youth fellowship.

In the early twentieth century came the InterVarsity Fellowship (later to be called UCCF) to support groups of evangelical students at university. Once again, its impact on the history of evangelicalism has been immense: 'Some of those prominent in leadership of churches, missionary societies and other Christian institutions of many varieties were first spiritually awakened and led to Christ in a University or College Christian Union. They learnt first to take responsibility in active service for Christ when serving on the committee of their student Christian Union.'[9]

IVF was also the birthplace of the Tyndale Fellowship for Biblical Research, which was instrumental in fostering a new generation of evangelical scholars who have in turn shaped evangelical thinking over the period. Another youth work movement, Crusaders, saw among its converts influential figures like Michael Saward and Bishop John Taylor.

Although Ward limits the focus of his research to evangelical Anglicanism, the principle that youth work shapes the future of the church has strong support elsewhere. Clive Calver, who for the last ten years has been hugely influential as head of the Evangelical Alliance, started out with British Youth For Christ. Many of Steve Chalke's now international media projects were experimented with as a youth minister at Tonbridge Baptist, and it was the ministry of Youth For Christ which also provided the support behind a young evangelist who was to go on to be quite influential – Billy Graham!

ADOLESCENT EVANGELICALISM

Not all of youth work's influence has been entirely positive, however. A variety of writers have noted unhelpful characteristics among Evangelicals that can be described as adolescent, perhaps as a result of drawing on its youth work roots.

For example, an over-emphasis on simplicity and certainty (so failing to do justice to the mystery and paradox in God's word), an intolerance of those who hold differing views, an authoritarian morality and an unhealthy focus on leadership. All, when analysed, have a genuine 'youthy' feel about them. Is it any wonder, asks Ward, that spirituality which has been so deeply influenced by work among young people is experiencing problems when it seeks to be relevant to older people?[10]

BASH'S UNINTENDED CONSEQUENCE

As a pioneering and successful model, the Bash camp had its imitators, but once again, as so often in history, the imitators copied the effect and lost the heart of the original. The camps' great strengths can be seen to become evangelicalism's great weaknesses in future generations. Strong Bible teaching and theological correctness in the rarefied atmosphere of camp became a tradition of theologically correct but largely un-applied evangelical teaching.

Many of these early youth work models were also specifically targeted at the privileged classes, with all the cultural trappings of education and money. We are therefore left with methods and patterns of youth work which have evolved almost exclusively in the rarefied context of public school and Oxbridge life, and they have not travelled well. 'The history of youth fellow-ship work in England is therefore largely the story of a movement downwards[11], the successive leaders attempting to adapt approaches developed in work amongst the upper middle classes to those further down the social scale.'

PROTECTION

Ward also very helpfully reveals the hidden agenda that lies behind much church youth work. He observes that it is often parental concerns which first create the environment, both emotionally and financially, for youth workers to be appointed. The unspoken motive is that parents want to keep their teenagers safe. This has some significant consequences. First, one of the chief aims of Christian youth work is to keep Christian teenagers separate from their non-Christian peers and the non-Christian world. This in turn secondly encourages a whole evangelical sub-culture of alterna-tive music, books, holidays, etc. in which Christian teenagers can be kept safe. The ultimate irony of this protectionist agenda is that: 'The chief means for outreach amongst young people which is adopted by evangelical churches is also the means by which those who are not "suitable" are at the same time excluded.'[12]

We are being to a large extent shaped by our ministry among young people. This means that ministry among young people is one of the key creative places where evangelicalism will renew itself, or not, as the case may be. The future shape of the church is at stake and the church looks to those working with young people for answers.[13]

Even if Ward is only half right (and I for one think that he is a lot more right than that) the strategic significance of the church's work with young people is underlined. *If it has got us to where we are, it can lead us to where we want to be.*

Revival

Within many quarters of the church currently there is a renewed interest in and prayerful anticipation of revival. Even a cursory glance at revival history will reveal the prominent part that children and young people have played in such movements of God's Spirit. Brian Edwards, in his book *Revival*,[14] devotes a whole section to examples of this from around the world. In this country, Harry Sprange has written an exhaustive and thorough work on how Scotland's children have consistently been instrumental in all the periods of revival over three centuries.

'I have just come this morning from an enquiry meeting appointed especially for the children. Several hundreds were present and very many of them were in tears. I could but feel that the Spirit of God was present, convicting of Sin. The dear ministers seemed most hearty in their work.'[15]

A very remarkable feature of the movement showed itself in the case of a number of young school boys who started a meeting for prayer amongst themselves. Of such youths as were at this time savingly impressed, not a few subsequently went forth as missionaries to China, India and Africa, while others filled pulpits at home.[16]

Scottish revivals involved children at every level. They saw miraculous healings of young people, witnessed parents converted through their children, saw children going to school to 'fight for Jesus', witnessed children and young people leading prayer meetings alone and saw them publicly giving testimony to their new faith in Christ.

In 1868, in one such period of revival in Scotland, C. H. Spurgeon put his considerable weight behind the specialist children's meetings taking place. His words show great wisdom and insight into what was quite a controversial issue in his day:

Prayer meetings for boys and girls judiciously conducted will be of abundant service. There should always be an experienced lover of children at their head and then the fewer grown up persons tolerated in the room the better. When there are half a dozen praying children present, their earnest prayers and tears will be with those of their own age, the most potent instrumentality imaginable. Never fear precocity. There is much more danger of indifference and levity. Let wisdom and love preside... We have never developed the capabilities of youth as we should have done.[17]

Sprange's careful detailed study of Scotland's children and young people in revival deserves serious attention. If children and young people have been prominent in revivals of the past (during a period of history in which young people were far less influential than they are today), how much more strategic will their role be in any revival of the future? *Surely it's pure escapism to wait and pray for revival but not do anything to prioritise our work with children and young people now.*

The Jesus Movement

One of the reasons we must be ready next time is that we have missed it before.

The Jesus Movement in the 1960s was the hippy generation's response to the traditional Christian church. While it is dangerous to generalise about the movement (as it covered, for example, the breadth of theological conviction from ultra-charismatic to ultra-conservative), members were basically united in a belief that the traditional church had failed to live as Jesus taught. Especially in the USA they ran homes for between six and fifteen members (modelled around the hippy communes) and sought a better world system through living by the Book, trusting God and developing a simple lifestyle. Evangelistically, they were by far the most successful Christians of their day in reaching hippies for Christ, partly because they placed great emphasis on treating people with dignity and taking time to answer questions (a reaction against the fundamentalist proclamation preaching of the conservative Evangelicals), and partly because they had a characteristic straightforward no-nonsense approach to the message, e.g. boycott hell! One commentator said at the time, 'It could spell the beginning of a great spiritual revolution, comparable to the Reformation.'[18]

However, the irony was that while the Jesus Movement rejected the traditional church, it actually needed the traditional church's input. Its anti-intellectualism, its despising of those who earned money and its general blindness to its own hippy culture's conditioning all required balancing, and the traditional church was the only means of this happening. However, by and large this did not happen because neither the church nor the Jesus Kids could overcome their cultural barriers and as a result the movement dissipated over time.

While there has been a lasting legacy of the Jesus Movement in this country (including the Good News Bible, Graham Kendrick and Greenbelt) one cannot help thinking about what might have been if only cultural barriers could have been overcome for the sake of Christ.

> If we don't disciple these kids, if the Jesus Movement folds, it will be the church's responsibility. If we just bend, we will see the greatest revival there has ever been, but if this Jesus Movement does not go on, you can put it down to the church blew it.[19]

Historical cycles

There is one other pointer to the historical significance of youth work which I want to draw attention to.

Dr Mark Senter earned his PhD by researching the history of youth ministry in the United States. As many other historians and sociologists have done before him, he argues that history goes in cycles and that the history of youth ministry is no exception.

In his book *The Coming Revolution in Youth Ministry*, Senter traces cycles in the Sunday school movement of the 1820s, the Christian Endeavour movement of the 1880s and the Youth For Christ movement of the early twentieth century. He concludes: 'A study of history suggests we are about to see a fundamental departure from what we have understood to be youth ministry during the closing decades of the twentieth century.'[20]

He goes on to predict that this coming revolution will be led by youth workers, frustrated by the incumbrances of institutional religion, who break out and try something new.

Why is this essential for today's youth leaders to know? Because:

> In each of the previous cycles of youth ministry, the sharpest criticism has come from the professional clergy. … the coming revolution will [again] generate extensive criticism.[21]

If Senter is right, history is in danger of repeating itself. We saw with the Jesus Movement a new move of God, but its enormous potential was lost because the church could not drop its cultural baggage enough to help refine and focus the vision. Youth congregations have a wonderful potential to engage a new generation for the gospel. Let us not make the same mistake again.

Summary of Chapter 14

Young people are an immediate priority for all Christian leaders because of the way they dynamically impact church life with vision, energy and growth.

Young people are a strategic priority for all Christian leaders because of the way youth work powerfully shapes the church of the future.

Young people are now a critical issue for all Christian leaders. The emergence of controversial youth congregations requires that we lay aside our own cultural baggage and come alongside young people in our churches for the sake of the gospel.

Conclusion

So what will it take to see this partnership between the church and young people?

The apostle Peter was not known for his humility – far from it – and for a strong, dogmatic man like him, following Jesus had been a hard, breaking journey. His cowardice and betrayal had been very public, of course, but there were also the subsequent struggles and conflicts as God slowly rid him of all his Jewish prejudice and the full implications of the gospel only slowly dawned on him.

But by the time Peter neared the end of his life, he had learned his lesson: 'To the elders among you ... Be shepherds of God's flock that is under your care, serving as overseers ... Young men, in the same way be submissive to those who are older. *All of you, clothe yourselves with humility towards one another, because, "God opposes the proud but gives grace to the humble"'* (1 Pet 5:1–5, my italics).

In these verses lies the key to safeguarding the essential role that young people can play in the church. It is very simple, it is the way of Christ, it is one word: humility.

It is the word to which the missionaries have

returned time and time again. When the Lausanne Congress published their report on reaching people of different cultural groups, they made the following points about the need for humility.[1] All Christians need:

- the humility to recognise that we are all prisoners of our own culture;
- the humility to understand and appreciate the culture to whom we go;
- the humility to begin where people are, not where we would like them to be;
- the humility to recognise that the best of us will not communicate as well as a trained local indigenous person;
- the humility to trust the Holy Spirit, without whom our witness is futile;
- the humility to follow Christ in renouncing and sacrificing the things of our background;
- in humility to identify with people of a different background.

It is therefore fitting that this book should end with a call to the church for humility towards young people made by one of the greatest missionaries of the modern age. The last word goes to Lesslie Newbigin.[2]

I have often heard people say that youth work is very important because the young people of today are the leaders of tomorrow. But this is surely the wrong way to look at the matter. We have to be concerned about young people not because they will be old later on, but because they are young now!

What really is at issue in this tension between age and youth? Is it not this, that the experience of us who are old, the experience which we think is our greatest asset in comparison with the young is a sinful experience, an experience full of compromise with the world, the flesh and the devil? The point is that we must have young people in the church because we must listen to them, because they have something to say to us, because they put radical questions to us about the way we have conformed to this world.

The tension between young and old in the church can be a fruitful tension if we follow the advice of St Peter and clothe ourselves – young and old alike – with humility, so that we can really listen to each other. Only a church which does that will find the secret of constant renewal.

Notes

Chapter 1

1. The Willowbank Report (Lausanne Commission for World Evangelization, 1978), p.7.
2. Roy McCloughry, *Tomorrow's World* (Christian Institute Lectures, 1996).
3. Mike Starkey, *Fashion and Style* (Monarch, 1995), pp.23–24.
4. George Gerbner quoted in Reynolds R. Ekstrom, *Pop Culture* (Don Bosco Multimedia, 1989), p.32
5. E. Peterson, *The Message* (Navpress, 1993), p.386.
6. The Willowbank Report (LCWE), p.20.

Chapter 2

1. Tom Sine, 'The Wrong Dream', *Tear Times*, Autumn 1996, p.15.
2. Dave Tomlinson, *The Post-Evangelical* (Triangle Books, 1995), p.41.
3. Phillips and Okholm, *Christian Apologetics in a Post Modern World* (IVP).
4. Os Guinness.
5. Tony Walter, *A Long Way From Home* (Exeter: Paternoster, 1979).
6. Os Guinness, *The Gravedigger File* (Hodder & Stoughton, 1983), p.74.
7. Os Guinness, *op. cit.*, p.91.
8. Cyprian, *The Lapsed* 11.
9. John Stott, *Issues Facing Christians Today* (Marshall Morgan & Scott, 1984), ch. 12.
10. Tom Sine, *Taking Discipleship Seriously.*
11. Tom Sine, 'The Wrong Dream', *Tear Times*, Autumn 1996, p. 15.
12. Catherine Booth, *Aggressive Christianity* (The Salvation Army S & P Department, re-published 1986), p.9.
13. 'Engaging the Culture', *Alpha Magazine*, October 1994.

14. Martyn Eden (ed), *Britain on the Brink* (Crossway Books, 1993), p.8.
15. Peter Wagner quoted by Alison Burnett in *Alpha* article on Willow Creek 1993.
16. Bishop Kenneth Cragg, *The Call of the Minaret* (Lutterworth, 1956). Quoted by John Stott, *Christian Mission in the Modern World* (Kingsway, 1986), p.123.

Chapter 3

1. Lesslie Newbigin, *Foolishness to the Greeks* (SPCK, 1985), ch. 1.
2. Lesslie Newbigin in Jock Stein (ed.), *Mission and the Crisis of Western Culture* (Handel Press, 1989), p.2.
3. Thom Hopler, *A World of Difference* (IVP, 1981), p.185.

Chapter 4

1. John Macquarrie, *Principles of Christian Theology* (London: SCM, 1966).
2. The Hittite Suzerain Treaty, for example.
3. Gavin Reid, *The Gagging of God* (IVP, 1969).
4. The Lausanne Covenant, para. 10, quoted in the Willowbank Report (LCWE, 1978), p.5.

Chapter 5

1. Robert Browning.
2. J. Richard Middleton and Brian J. Walsh, *Truth Is Stranger Than It Used to Be* (SPCK), Conclusion.
3. The World Council of Churches, Uppsala.

Chapter 6

1. Martin Robinson, *A World Apart* (Monarch).
2. John Ellis in Michael Eastman (ed.), *Inside Out* (Falcon Press, 1976), p.25.
3. C. S. Lewis, *Letters to Malcolm* (Collins, 1963). Quoted by John Stott, *Christian Mission in the Modern World* (Kingsway, 1986), p.13.

4. Alvin Toffler, *Future Shock* (Bodley Head, 1970). Quoting Stuart Berg Flexner, Senior Editor of the Random House Dictionary of the English Language.
5. Terry Dunnel, 'Spirituality, Culture and Young People' in *Frontier Youth Magazine*.
6. *Parents of Pupils Magazine* (Luton Churches Education Trust), issue no. 2.
7. Gordon Bailey in Gaukroger and Cohen, *How to Close Your Church in a Decade* (Scripture Union, 1992), p.100.

Chapter 7

1. *Daily Telegraph*, October 1996 quoted in *The Week* Magazine, 12 October 1996, p.14.
2. The AIDS Quarterly Surveillance Table, December 1993.
3. John Coleman, *Key Data on Adolescence* (TSA Ltd, 1997), p.50.
4. 'Reaching Young People of a Younger Age' – A Youth For Christ Triennial Convocation, 1994.
5. John Coleman, *op. cit.*, p.22.
6. Gallup Survey of 1,000 14- to 19-year-olds in 1992.
7. 1993 Public Health Report.
8. 1994 report by the Government's Chief Medical Officer.
9. *The Independent*, 23 January 1995.
10. 1994 Mori Poll.
11. Masuel M. Haghughi, Honorary Professor of Psychology at Hull University, writing in *The Independent*, April 1993.
12. Peter Wilson, 'The Impact of Cultural Changes on the Internal Experience of the Adolescent', *The Journal of Adolescence*, Vol. 11, issue 4, December 88.

Chapter 8

1. Peter Drucker, *Post Capitalist Society* (Butterworth/Heinemann), p.16.
2. Vice President Al Gore, *Earth in the Balance* (Plume Books), p.170.
3. Lesslie Newbigin, *Foolishness to the Greeks* (SPCK, 1985), ch. 5.
4. David Lyon, *The Steeple's Shadow* (SPCK [O/P]).
5. M. P. M. Richards, 'Parental Divorce and Children', LJRC data, Archive Bulletin no. 51, September 1992, p.7.

6. Gavin McGrath, *NB Magazine* (UCCF), issue 4.

7. Mike Starkey, *Fashion and Style* (Monarch, 1995), p.187.

8. Reynolds R. Ekstrom, *Pop Culture* (Don Bosco Multimedia, 1989).

9. Andrew Walker, *Telling the Story: Gospel Mission and Culture* (SPCK), quoted in *Leading Light Magazine*, vol. 3/1, Summer 1996.

10. Dean Borgman, 'Youth Culture and the Media', *Perspectives* (Baptist Youth Ministry Magazine), issue 13, Spring 1995.

11. S. Gaukroger and Cohen, *How to Close Your Church in a Decade* (Scripture Union, 1992), p.80.

12. Phil Wall, 'The Exodus of the Young', *Salvationist Magazine*.

13. Dr John Habgood, 'Culture of Contempt', in *Leading Light Magazine*, Vol. 3/1, Summer 1996, p.7.

14. Bill Gates, 'Creating the Global Information Society', a Microsoft White Paper, 1995, p.7.

15. This is the argument of Os Guinness, *The Gravedigger File* (Hodder & Stoughton, 1983), p.101.

16. Michael Grove in *The Times*, 24 June 1996.

17. Leslie Francis in *British Journal of RE*, vol. 14, no. 3.

18. Carl Henry, quoted in 'Reaching This Generation', Brainstormers training video 1994.

19. Dave Tomlinson, *The Post-Evangelical* (Triangle Books, 1995), p.75.

20. Zygmunt Bauman quoted by Roy McCloughry, *Tomorrow's People* (Christian Institute Lectures, 1996).

Chapter 9

1. Vincent Donovan.

2. John Stott.

3. Johnny Baker, 'Enculturalising the Gospel' (BYFC Position Paper, 1995).

4. Steve Turner quoted in David Lyon, *The Steeple's Shadow* (SPCK).

5. Lynn Franks in *The Times*, 24 June 1996.

6. Clive Calver, *Thinking Clearly About the Truth* (Monarch).

7. Lesslie Newbigin, interviewed in YFC vision document 1993.

8. J. Richard Middleton and Brian J. Walsh, *Truth Is Stranger Than It Used to Be* (SPCK).

9. Dave Tomlinson, *The Post-Evangelical* (Triangle Books, 1995), p.88.
10. Gavin Reid, *The Gagging of God* (IVP, 1969).
11. Charles Pickstone in *The Times*, 24 June 1996.
12. This is the philosophy of the Damaris Project, which aims to help Christian leaders to unmask the gods of this world.
13. Thom Hopler, *A World of Difference* (IVP, 1981), p.136.

Chapter 10

1. Anon.
2. Phillips and Okholm, *Christian Apologetics in a Post-Modern World* (IVP).
3. Os Guinness, *The Gravedigger File* (Hodder & Stoughton, 1983), p.82
4. Mike Breen, *Outside In* (Scripture Union, 1993), Bob Mayo, *Gospel Exploded* (Triangle Books, 1996), Pete Ward, *Youth Culture and the Gospel* (Marshall Pickering, 1992) have all documented this model of youth work.
5. Charles Finney quoted in Hofstadter, *Anti-intellectualism in American Life*, quoted in Os Guinness, *Fit Bodies, Fat Minds* (Hodder & Stoughton, 1995), p.64.
6. C. S. Lewis, 'Peace Proposals for Brother Every and Mr Bethel' in Walter and Hooper (eds), *Christian Reflections* (Fount Paperbacks, 1981), p.52.
7. Mike Starkey, *Fashion and Style* (Monarch, 1995), p.57.
8. J. C. Ryle, *Worldly Conformity* (1878), quoted by Os Guinness, *Fit Bodies, Fat Minds* (Hodder & Stoughton, 1995), p.65.
9. D. T. Niles, *A Treasury of Great Preaching* (Word, 1971), Vol. 12, p.188.
10. Howard Snyder, *Liberating the Church* (Marshall Pickering, 1983), quoted by Chris Seaton, *Your Mind Matters* (Word Books, 1993), p.68.
11. Roy McCloughry, *Tomorrow's World* (Christian Institute Lectures, 1996).

Chapter 11

1. A. J. Stott, 1805.
2. William Temple quoted by Michael Harper, *Let My People Grow*

(Logos International, 1977), p.66.

3. Gavin McGrath, *NB Magazine* (UCCF), June/July 1996.
4. John Holt, *How Children Fail* (Pelican Books).
5. Extracted and arranged from Gavin McGrath, *NB Magazine* (UCCF), June/July 1996.

Chapter 12

1. Michael Eastman, *Inside Out* (Falcon Books, 1976), p.18.
2. Vincent J. Donovan, *Christianity Rediscovered* (SCM Press Ltd, 1978), p.7 of Preface.
3. Bob Mayo, *Gospel Exploded* (Triangle Books, 1996), pp.39–40.
4. Priest, *Doing Theology with the Masai* (William Carey Library, 1990), p.208.
5. Bruce Olson, *Bruchko* (New Wine Press, 1973), p.141.
6. The Willow Bank Report (LCWE, 1978), p.9.
7. Don Richardson, *Peace Child* (Regal, 1974).
8. Bob Mayo, *Gospel Exploded* (Triangle Books, 1996), pp.42–43.
9. *The Times*, 25 June 1997.
10. Mackenzie and Mastra, *Mango Tree Church*, p.31, quoted by Ronald Sider in *Bread of Life* (Triangle Books, 1994), p.100.
11. The Willow Bank Report (LCWE, 1978).
12. Chuck Kraft.
13. Steve Gerali, *The Church and Youth Ministry* (Lynx Books, 1995), p.52.
14. Documented by Peter Schineller Jnr in the International Bulletin of Missionary Research, April 1996.

Chapter 13

1. Thom Hopler, *A World of Difference* (IVP, 1981), p.192.
2. A point originally made by the Willow Bank Report (LCWE, 1978), p.22.
3. Roland Allen, *Missionary Methods – St Paul's or Ours?* (London: Robert Scott, 1912). Reset with Memoir Eerdmans Publishing Co., 1962, p.81.
4. *Ibid.*
5. Vincent J. Donovan, *Christianity Rediscovered* (SCM Press, 1978), pp.15–16.
6. *Ibid.*, p.22.

7. Bob Mayo, *Gospel Exploded* (Triangle Books, 1996), p.9.

8. Vincent J. Donovan, *Christianity Rediscovered* (SCM Press, 1978), pp.15–16.

9. Roland Allen, *The Spontaneous Expansion of the Christian Church* (World Dominion Press, 1927, new edition 1962), pp.131–133.

10. Roland Allen, *Missionary Methods – St Paul's or Ours?*, p.143.

11. Laurence Singlehurst quoted in *Alpha Magazine*, Spring 1996.

12. Gordon Fee, expounding Romans 8 at the Scripture and Power of God Conference, HTB London, 19 June 1997.

13. Peter Ward, *Growing Up Evangelical* (SPCK, 1996).

14. *Ibid.*

15. Heather Evans, 'Missiological Principles for Youth Ministry' (dissertation) quoting Priest, *Doing Theology with the Masai* (William Carey Library, 1990), p.13.

16. Peter Ward, *Growing Up Evangelical* (SPCK, 1996), p.158.

17. *Youth Apart* (Church House Publishing, 1996).

Chapter 14

1. Leith Anderson, *Dying for Change* (Kingsway [Nova]).

2. George Barna, *Evangelism That Works* (New Wine Regal Books).

3. George Barna, *User Friendly Churches* (New Wine Regal Books), ch.11.

4. *Ibid.*

5. *Ibid.*

6. Anon.

7. Lesslie Newbigin, *Foolishness to the Greeks* (SPCK, 1985).

8. Alister McGrath quoted by Peter Ward, *Growing Up Evangelical* (SPCK, 1996), p.6.

9. Douglas Johnson, *Contending for the Faith*, p.301, quoted by Pete Ward, *op. cit.*, p.33.

10. Pete Ward, *op. cit.*, p.43.

11. *Ibid.*, p.45.

12. *Ibid.*, p.185.

13. *Ibid.*, p.216.

14. Brian H. Edwards, *Revival* (Evangelical Press, 1990).

15. *Word & Work*, 19 December 1862, quoted by Harry Sprange, *Kingdom Kids* (Christian Focus Publishing, 1994), p.108.

16. John Horn Reminiscences pp.48–49 quoted by Harry Sprange,

op. cit., p.167.

17. C. H. Spurgeon, *The Sword and the Trowel* (London, 1868), pp.149–150 quoted by Harry Sprange *op. cit.*

18. Roger C. Palms, *The Jesus Kids* (SCM Press, 1971).

19. Richard Hogue quoted by Roger C. Palms, *The Jesus Kids* (SCM Press, 1971).

20. Mark Senter III, *The Coming Revolution in Youth Ministry* (Victor Books, 1992), p.15.

21. *Ibid.*, p.181.

Conclusion

1. The Willow Bank Report (LCWE, 1978), pp.16–17.

2. I have taken the liberty of re-arranging the text though not the meaning of Newbigin's writing in Lesslie Newbigin, *The Good Shepherd* (The Faith Press, 1977), pp.83–84.